THINKING OUTSIDE THE OVEN

Concomitant Concepts and Synergistic Solutions for the Twenty-First Century

NED CONGER

iUniverse®

THINKING OUTSIDE THE OVEN
Concomitant Concepts and Synergistic Solutions
for the Twenty-First Century

iUniverse books may be ordered through booksellers or by contacting:

iUniverse
1663 Liberty Drive
Bloomington, IN 47403
www.iuniverse.com
1-800-Authors (1-800-288-4677)

Because of the dynamic nature of the Internet, any web addresses or links contained in this book may have changed since publication and may no longer be valid. The views expressed in this work are solely those of the author and do not necessarily reflect the views of the publisher, and the publisher hereby disclaims any responsibility for them.

Any people depicted in stock imagery provided by Thinkstock are models, and such images are being used for illustrative purposes only.
Certain stock imagery © Thinkstock.

ISBN: 978-1-5320-0123-9 (sc)
ISBN: 978-1-5320-0011-9 (e)

Library of Congress Control Number: 2016912068

Print information available on the last page.

iUniverse rev. date: 08/25/2016

CONTENTS

PREFACE

The nation and the world and all the living things that have preceded me over the past two million years have made possible for me a lifetime I have enjoyed immensely. Throughout this lifetime, I've tried to repay this state of happiness by battling the evil forces present on the earth and by contributing constructively to a wide variety of human activities, beginning with becoming a child picture frame maker in my father's photo studio at the age of twelve, followed by jobs as paperboy; dry goods clerk; small-town post office janitor; US Postal Service special delivery boy; curb-and-gutter-construction common laborer; farm harvester (shocker) of wheat, barley, and oats; farm laborer (on my uncle's dairy farm, including herding the cows to and from pasture and milking them, delivering milk, feeding pigs, gathering eggs, hoeing weeds in the cornfield, etc.); "gandy dancer" (common laborer on an emergency railroad-maintenance section gang restoring a thirty-mile stretch of railroad washed out by flood); cornet player in a dance band; funeral vocalist; small-town recreation director; substitute rural mail carrier; library page; house cleaner; house painter; fruit picker; fruit-cannery worker; furniture deliverer; brickyard worker; mason tender; and common laborer manufacturing freight cars. All these occupations occurred during my years in grade school, high school, and college, and with the exception of the tour in the Yankee Hill Brickyard moving bricks by wheelbarrow from the stiflingly hot kilns to freight cars, I enjoyed them all to a certain extent, realizing that they were just stepping-stones to more important careers.

These preparatory activities led to a twenty-two-year career in the US Navy, followed by a thirty-eight-year career as a program analyst/program manager/ consultant to the navy's F/A-18 Strike Fighter (Hornet, Super Hornet, Growler) program, the nation's most successful aircraft-system acquisition in terms of capability, performance, cost, and schedule. Throughout these last two careers, I experienced the satisfaction of having several of my ideas for improving the nation's defense capabilities implemented. This gave me the confidence to offer to you the following "half-baked ideas."

I would like to thank the following friends for editorial assistance and encouragement: Richard Gaskin, John Wells, Jane Shaffer, Karl Pecht, and Joseph Chrzanowski.

INTRODUCTION

My working title for this book was *Concomitant Concepts and Synergistic Solutions for the Twenty-First Century*. Since that sounds a bit grandiose, and in light of my experience in trying to interest those I considered to be my most logical collaborators in implementing these solutions, I relegated it to a subtitle. I hold great hopes that the book will turn out to be less of an avuncular whimsicality and more of a blueprint for the nation and the world to straighten themselves out.

I haven't conducted what I would consider to be thorough research on many of my concepts, but I have attempted to bring them to the attention of more qualified experts who might perceive the potential in these ideas for human benefit and might apply their qualifications, capabilities, and power to the concepts' fruition.

I consider myself a problem solver. It's not that I search for problems to solve, but when I become aware of them, I almost instinctively start thinking of ways to cure or at least ameliorate them. I have devoted a chapter to each of fifty-eight problems or situations for which I think I have a solution. In some cases, the ideas are less of the problem-solving category and could be described more accurately simply as opportunities to improve the nation's (or world's) quality of life. I am particularly fond of synergistic solutions where two or more of my ideas combine to solve a problem. I'm even more pleased with synergy in reverse, where more than one problem is solved by the same idea, sort of like getting two pheasants with one shot. Although in order to keep the book from appearing too ponderous, I have included solutions to several quite inconsequential problems or situations. Some of these could best be described as whimsical. The focus is on solutions of significant importance to the nation's (or world's) survival or at least comfort. You will probably consider some of them to be half-baked ideas, and I might agree with you, in that detailed and comprehensive studies have yet to be conducted in order to make sure further pursuit of them is likely to be successful and cost effective. I hope that this book will inspire those with the appropriate technical abilities to examine these ideas and perhaps pop them back into the oven. The problems needing solutions and ideas that just might help in resolving them, that I've given significant thought to, are:

1. countering global warming, acid rain, hurricanes, and tornadoes;
2. improving the marking of streets and highways;
3. advertising on the surfaces of streets and highways;
4. leasing the rights-of-way on interstate highways and other highways for the purpose of growing trees and other plants;
5. a revolutionary health care plan;
6. countering avian flu;
7. a step toward solving the energy problem: floating oil refineries;
8. improved fuel economy and safer, less stressful driving;
9. flood control and improving the world's water quality;
10. creating wetlands and recycling tires;
11. countering forest and brush fires while easing prison overcrowding and reducing air pollution;
12. countering illegal immigration with airborne assets;
13. restoration basketball;
14. aerospacers: an organization to improve training in science and technology;
15. combined stadium, hotel, and convention centers;
16. a revolution in television programming and advertising;
17. the interstate highway guide;
18. foot-treadle electric generators as accessories for computers;
19. a new political party capable of winning elections with little need for campaign financing;

49. reviving hydroelectric power;
50. improving fuel mileage in eighteen-wheelers;
51. ending the wars in Iraq, Syria, and Afghanistan with the big boom;
52. solving the Greek financial problem;
53. floating industrial island;
54. electricity from high-rise waste water;
55. off-loading container ships using heavy-lift helicopters;
56. countering illegal immigration;
57. a service that could be provided by street beggars; and
58. filling empty coal cars with garbage to be dumped in or near abandoned mines.

THE BEST WAY TO HAVE A GOOD IDEA IS TO HAVE LOTS OF IDEAS.

—LINUS PAULING

CHAPTER 1

GLOBAL WARMING, HURRICANES, TORNADOES, AND ACID RAIN

Global warming—these two words are of enormous concern to millions of managers, workers, and owners of businesses dependent to a substantial degree on the combustion of fossil fuels. They have spent billions of dollars and will probably be forced to spend hundreds of billions more in efforts to reduce the production of carbon dioxide and other greenhouse gases that are blamed by many "authorities" (elected and unelected) for the earth's current warming cycle that began in 1850. Some students of this warming trend, who may not see the greenhouse effect as its sole cause, believe it is contributing to the phenomenon, if not accelerating it.

The words *global warming* and *climate change* strike fear in the minds of millions of inhabitants of the earth who have seen or heard about increasingly pessimistic reports such as the documentary film *An Inconvenient Truth* produced by former vice president Al Gore. My solution to the problem of global warming will be far less expensive and far more effective than any plan currently in effect or on the drawing boards.

In 1974 I began to study the cycles of global warming and global cooling. I was an officer on the staff of the commander, Naval Intelligence Command, and became interested in the strategic impacts of these phenomena. I was the director of the Naval Intelligence Command's Reserve Intelligence Program.

The personnel in this program included several hundred reservists who worked on intelligence projects one weekend a month and during a two-week period of active duty. I assigned these reservists—some of whom were scientists, college professors, and computer experts—projects for which they had excellent capabilities. I was always on the lookout for new areas on which to focus their skills.

At the time, there was actually more concern over global cooling than global warming, because in the 1940s there had been a slight interruption in the general warming cycle that had begun in 1850. In 1974 a report prepared by the Central Intelligence Agency on global cooling came to my attention, and it prompted me to look for possible projects for the reservists. A few meteorologists and climatologists and many alarmists eager to attach themselves to the latest looming disaster feared the return of the Little Ice Age, a global cooling cycle that occurred between 1580 and 1850. What might the strategic implications of such an occurrence have on the relative military capabilities of the navies of the United States and the Soviet Union? For that matter, what had been the strategic and tactical implications of the Little Ice Age?

I had completed nine years at sea aboard aircraft carriers, operating primarily in the warm waters of the Mediterranean Sea and the South China Sea, with short sojourns to the North Atlantic and Northern Pacific, and had talked with other navy men who had more experience in cold-water operations. Very definitely a severe cooling trend would be to the disadvantage of carrier operations, in that ice on the flight decks, aircraft, and associated equipment make operating in arctic waters far more hazardous than is the case in warmer seas. A sailor falling overboard in the Mediterranean Sea or the South China Sea could be rescued many hours after the event, but a similar mishap in the northern waters would result in death from hypothermia within minutes.

I began my research with an examination of what the strategic and tactical military implications had been during the Little Ice Age. Actually they had been quite consequential.

In the mid-seventeenth century, the king of Sweden yearned to conquer Denmark, primarily to stop the Danes from exacting tribute from ships transiting the straits that separated the two nations and connected the Baltic

Sea with the North Sea. The Swedish king had an army superior to that of Denmark but hadn't been able to produce a navy capable of defeating the Danes at sea, much less land an amphibious force in Denmark. But in 1658, with the Little Ice Age at its coldest, the straits separating the two nations froze to a thickness strong enough to allow Sweden's army of seven thousand men, complete with cavalry, artillery, and supply wagons, to march across the straits and defeat the Danes. That same winter the residents of Manhattan Island had no need for a Staten Island ferry either, in that they could walk on the ice between the islands.

The Soviet Union's greatest threat to the United States Navy in 1974 was its very impressive submarine fleet, based primarily near the Arctic Circle in Murmansk and Vladivostok. I speculated that since these bases were much farther north than the straits separating Sweden and Denmark, a repetition of the Little Ice Age might very well freeze the waters of the far north to a thickness that would make the Soviet submarine bases unusable, despite the best efforts of Soviet icebreakers. The Soviet Union would be forced to rely on its Black Sea submarine bases. But with the exit to the Mediterranean Sea surrounded by Turkey and Greece, nations friendly to the United States, the Soviet submarine threat would virtually disappear.

What was the likelihood of a return of the Little Ice Age? What caused it? Could similar conditions occur again? Since significant tactical advantages might accrue to the US Navy vs. the Soviet submarine fleet, might it be advisable to accelerate a cooling period?

Many climatologists believe the warming and cooling of the earth is affected by changes in the sun's output, with periods of high solar flare or sunspot activity. These could be followed by warm periods on the earth and periods of low sunspot activity, followed by cool periods. Other scientists believe that since these changes occur more frequently than changes in relatively long warming or cooling cycles, they are less likely to cause long-term change than other phenomena, such as changes in the earth's orbit around the sun, changes in the inclination of the earth toward the sun, and changes in the earth's magnetic poles. Former speaker of the house Newt Gingrich offered these influences as far more responsible for warming cycles than human activities so dramatically displayed by former vice president Al Gore in his documentary. A few authorities think tectonic-plate activity, particularly on the floor of the Pacific Ocean, resulting in extrusions of quantities of molten lava, has some effect, possibly causing the warm periods called El Niño and the cool periods, La Niña. Still others believe that greenhouse effects caused by stratospheric concentrations of carbon dioxide and other gases are to blame. There is less agreement on whether human activity causes these cycles, but an increasing number of scientists and other students of weather trends— particularly those who benefit economically from agreeing with the alarmists, via grants, and so on—believe that the warming trend has been influenced by a greenhouse effect intensified by the burning of fossil fuels.

Regardless of the basic cause of global cooling, it appears that a cooling trend begins with a series of winters in which there is an early and extensive snowfall in the Northern Hemisphere. With a greater-than-usual area of the land covered by snow, more of the sun's rays are reflected back into space rather than absorbed by the bare ground. This process, referred to in scientific circles as albedo, results in approximately 90 percent of the sun's rays being reflected from the snow back into space. After several winters of increasingly cold temperatures over increasingly longer periods of time, each long winter seems to replicate itself in a sort of snowball effect. Then the snowfields and glaciers expand, and a cooling cycle begins.

In order to expedite a return to a Little Ice Age and therefore deprive the Soviet Union of its Arctic submarine bases, I suggested, half in jest, that we cover large areas of land in North America and Western Europe with nontoxic white substances, to simulate early and extensive snow cover exhibited at the outset of global cooling periods. As you may have observed, my suggestion wasn't taken seriously, and with further research, I discovered that due to a warm ocean current branched off from the Gulf Stream, at least the Soviet submarine base at Murmansk was likely to stay ice free, even during a very cold cycle. So, without involving my highly qualified intelligence reservists in a project to come up with a plan to expedite global cooling, I abandoned my campaign to bring about a return of the Little Ice Age.

However, when a few years later the threat of global warming replaced the potential calamity of global cooling, I began to think my idea for sending more of the sun's rays back into space could have slowed or even stopped global warming, had it been implemented back in 1974 and then expanded regularly over subsequent years, even though it hadn't been necessary to use it strategically against the Soviet submarine fleet.

My current idea is to cover a substantial area of undeveloped land as well as agricultural fields around the world with a thin coat of lime, white sand, kaolin (a soft, white, claylike mineral), a reflective polyethylene mulch, or other white nontoxic substance, thus replicating the effect of an early snowfall. The white substances would have definite advantages over an early snowfall in their ability to reflect sunlight. Unlike snow, these substances would not disappear in the spring. If lime were used for this purpose, it would eventually be absorbed into the soil or washed into waterways and then replaced as necessary. Since thousands of acres of farmland and forests are currently degraded from the effects of acid rain, absorption of lime would be beneficial, not only to the fields being treated but to streams, ponds, and lakes receiving the resultant alkaline runoff. Many of these waterways are so acidic today that they are no longer inhabited by fish and other wildlife dependent on them. The states of New York and West Virginia and sportsmen's clubs and other organizations interested in reclaiming streams and ponds in the United States Northeast have already been adding lime directly to streams and ponds to counter the ill effects of acid rain.

Spreading lime or other white substances over agricultural land after it has been seeded, but just before the plants have sprouted and thus not interfering with germination, may have other beneficial effects. Because the sun's rays striking the white surface would be reflected outward at various angles, rather than being absorbed in the untreated earth, the emerging plants would receive a double dose of sunlight. Experiments have shown that plants that have received greater-than-normal exposure to ultraviolet rays are less susceptible to attack by insects. A reflective polyethylene mulch is already being applied to the soil in a few fruit orchards in the United States in order to achieve a more uniform ripe coloring of the fruit through the reflected sun rays.

Additional reflected sunlight could not only help plants resist insects but accelerate the process of photosynthesis, causing them to mature more quickly, lessening the time of exposure to hungry herbivores and omnivores, drought, hailstorms, and early fall freezes. This program could therefore have favorable impacts on crop yields. In areas where lime is determined to be an undesirable component to the soil, another white, insoluble, and nontoxic substance could be applied. A similar nontoxic substance able to float on water in powder, granular, or liquid form could be spread over large, deep-water ocean areas with little effect on submerged vegetation but would reflect the sun's rays back into space. This would allow these ocean areas to remain cooler than would otherwise be the case. This same substance applied to rice paddies at an appropriate time might give rice plants enough extra photosynthesis to mature more quickly with the same benefits outlined above for grains grown on dry land.

Concomitant benefits from spreading a white film over ocean areas might result in fewer and weaker hurricanes and typhoons. Some scientists have speculated that the intensity of recent hurricanes may have been increased by higher-than-usual temperatures in the Gulf of Mexico. Some of the cooling efforts I have in mind might even reduce the threat of tornadoes. (More on this later.)

It might take several years to determine the effect these techniques have on global warming, but effects of the acid-reducing lime applications would provide near-term benefits. International participation in this program would provide earlier evidence of its efficacy. Since acid rain is a problem in both Europe and Asia, the lime application would begin immediately to alleviate damage to the environment caused by acid rain.

Other techniques for reflecting sunlight could be applied in conjunction with the ground-whitening process. Roofs of both residential and commercial buildings could be painted white, adding to the reduction in heat-absorbing surfaces. Incentives such as income tax deductibility or tax credits could be initiated to encourage whitening of both ground and rooftop surfaces. California has already implemented such a program on a relatively small scale.

I have nothing against the various schemes designed to reduce the emissions of carbon dioxide and to improve air quality, but I think the scientists and their followers who propose them are attacking the symptoms of the problem rather than the problem itself.

Symptoms of the problem are warm gaseous particles in the atmosphere that have been transformed into their current heated state from a cooler existence on the earth's surface through collisions with particles speeding from the sun's core at the speed of light. If all combustion of fossil fuels suddenly came to a halt, global warming would still continue, unless something is done to prevent so many of the sun's high-speed particles from transforming less aggressive earth particles into hot little components of the atmosphere. This can be done easily by whitening significant areas of the earth, so that like the snow cover in winter, they can reflect these high-speed, global warming particles back into space before inflicting their damage on the earth.

I have been trying for several years to interest the federal government, the United Nations, and other entities capable of implementing this plan for countering global warming, with no response. So without governmental assistance in whitening the earth, I've tried to develop incentives for independent participation by owners of land areas and other surfaces that could be whitened. If farmers and others engaged in agriculture can be convinced that whitening their fields will be cost effective, they might be willing to adopt this practice. A concomitant benefit could accompany any significant application of whitening to agricultural fields. Since whitened ground would be cooler than the presumably larger areas of adjacent untreated ground, a weather condition similar to the coastal sea breeze effect should develop. With the cooler air above the whitened fields moving outward toward the untreated fields, warmer air above these fields would rise. Depending on the extent of the whitened fields, the cool breezes thus produced might inhibit the forming of tornadoes. A small town, with all its roofs painted white, surrounded by acres of whitened fields, might be less vulnerable to tornadoes.

I realize that this idea will encounter considerable skepticism. John Locke predicted quite eloquently: "New opinions are always suspected and usually opposed, without any other reason but because they are not already common." But if the concept turns out to have potential for reducing global warming, hurricanes and tornadoes, and the effects of acid rain as well, it would eventually find support from those currently impacted by these effects, especially those living in areas where a future rising sea level can expect to have disastrous economic and social effects. Every industrial and individual consumer of fossil fuel stands to benefit from this concept through the relaxation of costly efforts to slow the greenhouse effect. Concomitant improvements in agricultural productivity and wildlife habitat constitute an additional bonus.

If at first this proposed solution seems ridiculous, remember the words of Albert Camus, Nobel Laureate in literature: "All great deeds and all great thoughts have a ridiculous beginning."

THE TIME HAS COME TO WHITEN THE EARTH.

CHAPTER 2

IMPROVING THE MARKING OF STREETS AND HIGHWAYS

The central idea of this chapter, as well as chapter 3, even while proposing ideas that will make automotive travel more convenient for drivers and providing new sources of income for governmental entities, will synergistically assist in accomplishing the objective of chapter 1. This is because the concepts examined in these two chapters result in paint or other substances being applied to the surfaces of streets and highways, thus reflecting more of the sun's rays back into space rather than allowing them to be absorbed in black highway surfaces, where they contribute to global warming.

Chapter 2 is simply the outline of a campaign to make greater use of the surfaces of streets and highways to display driving directions and speed limits. From an office I had in Arlington, Virginia's Crystal City, I frequently walked to the Pentagon, about a kilometer distant. During at least one out of every five trips, an automobile, usually one with an out-of-state license, would pull up alongside me, and the driver or passenger would ask me for directions: to Washington, to Richmond, to Arlington Cemetery, to Alexandria, to Interstate 95, and several other destinations or way points. I finally developed a little map of the area with directions on it to the most common destinations and then ran off copies to hand to confused motorists whenever I was asked for directions.

It occurred to me that even drivers of automobiles with global positioning systems and audible driving instruction features would benefit from frequent displays on the road surface, such as arrows followed by brief messages, for example, "To I-95," "To Arlington Cemetery," and so forth. Speed limits would also be displayed on the road surface. There was a stretch of one highway near the Pentagon where the speed limit dropped abruptly, with only a small roadside sign, easily missed by a driver trying to read other overhead and roadside signs. This turned it into an unintentional speed trap. Speed limits should be displayed on the road surface at least three times immediately following a change in the limit, and at least once in every subsequent mile.

My business once took me to the General Electric Aircraft Engine facility in Lynn, Massachusetts, just north of Boston. Hosts at General Electric had provided me a detailed set of travel instructions, which directed the driver to follow a particular Massachusetts highway route, with several turns in its meandering path through Boston and Lynn to General Electric. Watching out for traffic lights and avoiding collisions with faster-moving vehicles, I missed at least two of these turns and had to make an expanding square search each time to relocate the highway. If that highway had had its route number emblazoned on the surface at least once in each block, just before turns and immediately following each turn, I'd have been able to find my way through Lynn quite easily.

This type of street and highway marking system will have concomitant benefits in addition to ameliorating global warming and making it easier for motorists to locate and follow a desired route. It should result in less fuel wasted by lost motorists in relocating their paths. It will reduce road rage in motorists easily upset by any impedance in their routes. It will reduce fights and accidents caused by such road rage, as well as accidents where motorists have entered one-way streets inadvertently or interstate highways from the wrong direction. Perhaps best of all, it will tend to keep motorists' eyes on the road rather than searching for roadside signs. This will certainly reduce the number of rear-end accidents.

By shifting road signs from roadside or overhead locations to the road surfaces, there will be less obstruction of scenic views. In populated areas it would be advantageous to have the street names displayed at least once in each direction each block, with street numbers displayed on the street surface in front of each residence or business.

Chapter 3 will expand upon the philosophy introduced here and will provide a means for financing the proposed highway marking system.

> DO NOT QUENCH YOUR INSPIRATION AND YOUR IMAGINATION.
> —VINCENT VAN GOGH

CHAPTER 3

ADVERTISING ON THE SURFACES OF STREETS AND HIGHWAYS

Like the concept outlined in chapter 2, the following proposal has synergistic and concomitant qualities in common with my ideas for countering global warming. Surfaces of streets and highways should be used for advertising. A portion of the advertising revenues would be made available to the government entities responsible for the highway-marking program outlined in chapter 2 and used for this purpose. Road-surface advertising will be especially useful for motorists on interstate highways and other limited-access routes, where today the principal means of advertising products and services available at individual exits are relatively small groups of roadside announcements a short distance from certain exits. It is sometimes difficult for the motorist to pick out the product or service desired, as the sign is frequently passed at relatively high speed and occasionally blocked by vehicles in the outside lane. Having to read these signs at night, with little or no illumination, aggravates the problem.

Allowing the businesses with services near the approaching exit to present this information tastefully and clearly on the road surface several times before each exit will be of great convenience to the motorists and will match customers and vendors far more efficiently than is the case today. The surfaces within five miles of each exit should be reserved for businesses located near the exit. The rest of the highway surfaces could be made available to more distant businesses such as motels and restaurants and to general advertising of food products, beverages, fuel, and the like.

The paints used for this type of advertising should be of sufficient graininess so as not to adversely affect the highway braking surface. The paints in use today marking highway lanes would be suitable for use in these advertisements. In keeping with the synergistic theme of this book, it should be noted that all these advertisements will reflect more of the sun's rays back into space during the day and thus assist in the campaign to counter global warming.

Although white paint would be preferable for as many advertisements as possible because of its reflectivity and readability on dark surfaces, nationally known brands with unique and well-known color schemes, such as the red background for Coca-Cola or the green background for Holiday Inn should also be authorized.

Opponents of this idea will complain that the very process of painting the road surfaces will be too much of a traffic hindrance to tolerate. This problem can be alleviated by permitting the advertisers to implant their messages primarily at the same time that the highway lane markers are being renewed.

Skeptics of the idea that applying paint to street and highway surfaces can assist in countering global warming might be willing to assist in cost/benefit research, comparing the relative merits of these processes with efforts of equal cost devoted to replacing incandescent lightbulbs with fluorescent bulbs or replacing gasoline with ethanol. The amount of global warming rays of sunlight reflected back into space by a dollar's worth of white paint can be quantified far more precisely than can the amount of global warming reduced by a dollar's worth of lightbulbs or a dollar's worth of ethanol, yet millions of environmentalists eagerly embrace the latter two processes with unquestioning fervor.

> LIFE IS A GREAT BIG CANVAS, AND YOU SHOULD
> THROW ALL THE PAINT ON IT YOU CAN.
> —DANNY KAYE

CHAPTER 4

Tree-Lined Interstate Highways and Other Highways

This project has the potential for achieving a multitude of valuable benefits to the citizenry of the United States. It will give the individual states and their inhabitants a new source of income through a process that will, at the same time, help reduce greenhouse gases, improve highway safety, reduce snow-removal costs, purify the air, reduce the frequency and severity of highway accidents, bring new industry to the states, and add to the states' aesthetic beauty.

I've had the idea of leasing the highway medians and rights of way for the purpose of growing trees for some time and have been trying to interest the federal government (Department of Interior, EPA, US Forest Service) in this plan for the past several years. You can't imagine the bureaucratic maze I have encountered. I finally got a phone call from someone from the US Forest Service, who told me it was a good idea, but his impression was that the states are now trying to cut down any trees in the divided-highway medians, to avoid lawsuits from automobile owners who crashed into them. You will see in my plan, on the next pages, how I would approach that objection. However, if the auto crash potential is too difficult to overcome, commercially beneficial bushes and plants with extensive root structure could be substituted. They would provide many of the benefits of trees but would only slow down the crashing cars, rather than bring them to an abrupt halt.

Several years ago, on a flight from Washington, DC, to Lincoln, Nebraska, I happened to sit by the senior official of the US Forest Service in Nebraska, and I described my plan to him and told him I was trying to interest the federal government in it. He liked the idea, and we discussed the best species for such a program in Nebraska. He noted that there was a new rapid-growth poplar or cottonwood hybrid that would be especially suitable.

The plan is to lease to individuals, organizations, and private businesses the highway rights of way of the interstate highway system and other highways, for the purpose of growing trees. Leases of varying time periods on currently treeless segments of these highways would be awarded to the highest bidder at well-publicized public auctions. This plan has several concomitant benefits, which are listed below.

1. This plan will have an appreciable effect on the reduction of carbon dioxide in the environment and therefore assist in countering the greenhouse aspects of global warming. Trees, bushes, and other plants love carbon dioxide and are excellent carbon traps. These stands of trees and other greenery will flourish in their proximity to one of the greatest sources of this gas—automobiles.

2. Significant monetary resources will accrue to the states from the leasing of these segments. Some of these funds might be set aside for maintenance of these new forests (e.g., irrigation, pruning, pest control, etc.), in that having these activities performed by professionals would result in healthier and safer forests. However, considering the current financial condition of most of the states, perhaps these funds are better applied to education or to the overall deficit, leaving the cost of maintaining and nurturing the stands of trees to the lessees.

3. Individuals and institutions such as mutual funds, pension plans, insurance companies, banks, and foreign nations may shift some of their more conservative funds to this relatively safe investment from less dependable and riskier endeavors. The state forest services would provide estimates of the times of maturity and values at harvest for the various species and should probably have something to say about recommended species to be planted in the various locations.

4. Some years hence, there will be a continuous new source of lumber and other wood products in participating states. It will be located very favorably for harvest and for transport to lumber mills. It is possible that new furniture companies, paper mills, and other businesses will develop in locales where these resources were not previously available.

5. Across the east-west highways of the northern states, these belts of trees would serve well as snow fences, making the winter maintenance of the highways less expensive and easier for road crews. Admittedly, there will be areas where, during blizzards, the snowdrifts will extend from the tree line onto the highway, but the maintainers would see this developing and be prepared to cope with it.

6. From an aesthetic and scenic aspect, this plan will bring about significant improvement to the landscape and make trips through formerly desolate country more agreeable.

7. From a safety standpoint, trees in the median will be of benefit in two important ways: they will shield drivers' eyes from oncoming lights in the opposite lanes at night, and they will provide a barrier to the occasional automobile that goes out of control and crosses the median into oncoming traffic. If, as the US Forest Service has stated to me, there is concern that trees in the median could contribute to damage to automobiles departing the highway, trees such as fir, spruce, pine, cedar and Leyland cypress might be planted in these areas. They would assist in reducing glare from oncoming headlights and would slow down automobiles before they crossed the median and collided with oncoming traffic but would not provide a solid enough shock when struck to cause serious injury to the car's occupants.

8. This program will provide excellent opportunities for the states' governors and other officials to develop and maintain good relationships with county and other local officials, appearing at auctions, tree plantings, and so on.

9. Since in some areas of many states there is high unemployment, this program will provide thousands of full-time and part-time jobs. In the near term, many of these will be on tree farms, growing far more seedlings than has been the case in recent experience. Next will come

tree-planting and cultivating jobs, and ultimately tree-harvesting and wood-processing jobs. Dozens of managerial, clerical, and support jobs will accompany development of the program.

10. Foreign investors may take an interest in this project, in that unlike their investments in US government bonds, they would be the owners of trees that, unlike the dollar, would increase in value each year.

Unlike most federal and state projects of this magnitude, this one will not be a burden to taxpayers. On the contrary, it will be a source of considerable income to the participating states.

WE ARE CONTINUALLY FACED BY GREAT OPPORTUNITIES BRILLIANTLY DISGUISED AS INSOLUBLE PROBLEMS.
—LEE IACOCCA

CHAPTER 5

SOLVING TWO OF THE NATION'S BIGGEST PROBLEMS SIMULTANEOUSLY: HEALTH CARE AND SAVINGS

With US auto manufacturers nearly driven into bankruptcy and other American industries eliminated from international competition because of rising medical expenses for their workforce and retirees, it is time to rescue the US economy with a new approach to medical care.

This plan would provide medical care while building personal savings accounts. It would eliminate the need for medical insurance programs including Obamacare, Medicare, and Medicaid. It would make it possible for every person in the country to obtain long-term care when necessary and at the same time provide an incentive to avoid unnecessary treatment. It would make the United States a more attractive site for foreigners seeking medical attention, thus creating additional high-skill jobs. It would revitalize American industry by relieving it of the burden of providing medical insurance. It would free the medical profession from governmental and HMO bureaucracies and would provide a new source of revenue for the federal government, thus reducing the necessity for international borrowing.

This plan is based on a 10 percent sales tax. Since medical expenses currently comprise 16 percent of the gross domestic product, and this plan would cover the majority of these expenses more efficiently, a 10 percent tax should be instituted initially, to be adjusted later as necessary as the current programs are phased out. This concept would result in every person paying a 10 percent sales tax at the time of every purchase. Each person would be provided a card similar to a credit card that would be processed at the time of the transaction. The 10 percent charge would be credited to the individual's medical savings plan and handled the same way credit card transactions are handled today.

When the individual needs medical attention, he or she would provide the card to the doctor, who would submit a claim to the agency handling the account and then be reimbursed directly. If the individual has insufficient funds in his or her medical savings account at the time of the charge, the agency would still pay the doctor but would enter a negative amount in the account, which would generally be worked off over subsequent years as the individual continues to pay into the account. At an age to be determined by actuaries, individuals would be permitted to withdraw funds from what they have saved, much as 401(k) withdrawals are handled today. These withdrawals would be tax free, even though the funds would have accumulated interest over the years. Funds remaining at the time of the individual's death would become part of the estate. The agency handling these accounts would use boards of doctors to make random checks of the amounts being charged, and severe penalties would be imposed on doctors and patients found to be cheating the system.

Businesses, institutions, and organizations would also pay the 10 percent tax. The money thus collected would be maintained in that entity's account and would be made available to the company to pay catastrophic medical expenses incurred by employees or consumers who have been injured by the company's products or actions, thus avoiding the necessity of lengthy litigation over such events. Companies could also use these funds for preventive medicine, maintaining their own preventive medical programs on site or conveniently nearby. This savings account would also be available to reimburse persons or institutions who suffer loss due to a company's bankruptcy. This fund would be required to be disbursed to shareholders and others who have lost money because of the company's failure, before the company is allowed to file for bankruptcy. For companies and institutions that accumulate excessive amounts in their medical savings accounts, there would be a provision for them to withdraw a certain percentage on an annual basis.

The government would pay interest on the funds in each medical savings account at a rate comparable to that paid on US savings bonds. The Social Security Administration or the Internal Revenue Service could handle the medical savings accounts, or a credit card company, such as Visa or MasterCard or one of the information-technology companies such as IBM or EDS could be contracted competitively.

Foreign citizens and businesses would also pay this tax and would be allowed to establish medical savings accounts similar to those of US citizens, but whereas the US citizen would be allowed to accrue a negative balance in his savings account, a foreign participant would be allowed access only to the amount that has actually accumulated.

Since funds being expended belong to the covered individual, there would be an incentive to obtain only necessary medical attention, avoiding unnecessary visits to emergency rooms and nonessential tests and procedures occurring today because the patients frequently are not the ones who bear the expense. The overall health of the nation would improve because people currently uninsured are receiving neither proper preventive care nor timely treatment of conditions that later land them in emergency rooms. There would no longer be any incentive for delaying a necessary visit to the doctor.

Some people may not want their purchases to be recorded, for fear that the IRS might be able to access the records and discover a lifestyle unsupported by reported income. These people could request that the tax they pay on selected purchases be credited to the general fund, rather than to their own medical account. These funds would help subsidize the needs of individuals whose accounts have temporary negative balances. These provisions would make it possible for people who are afraid of too much government intrusion into their private lives to opt out of reporting any specific purchases they desire to keep secret.

Of lesser importance, only to the fact that everyone in the United States would be provided medical care, is the lifting of the burden of medical insurance from American industry. This would make employers far more willing to create new jobs, relieving American businesses of a serious disadvantage not experienced by competitors worldwide. With foreign visitors and importers of American products accumulating large balances in their US medical savings plans, the already significant numbers of foreigners seeking medical care in the United States would multiply, making the nation the world's center of medical care.

With the removal of the medical care burden from US business, and the removal of the insurance compliance burden from doctors, hospitals, and laboratories, the US economy would enter an unprecedented period of expansion and prosperity.

I've discussed this plan with twenty-one physicians, and every one of them agrees that it would be a better plan than any other in effect or being proposed.

EVERYTHING SHOULD BE MADE AS SIMPLE AS POSSIBLE, BUT NOT SIMPLER.

—ALBERT EINSTEIN

CHAPTER 6

COUNTERING AVIAN FLU

Avian flu has faded in importance to the US news media, but its threat is still present in rural areas, principally in the Orient.

Medical researchers appear to be making progress toward producing vaccines and medications that may someday prevent or cure the disease, but it is unlikely that the United States or any other nation will be well prepared should there be an extensive outbreak of the disease in the near future.

Since avian flu would be spread throughout the population in many of the same ways that other strains of flu are spread, an experiment might be conducted during the current flu season that could lead to a set of measures that would help contain the spread of avian flu should it become epidemic in the United States.

This experiment could be conducted at relatively low expense by selecting two similar communities for study and encouraging the population of one of these communities to carry out a special antiflu campaign, while the population of the second community is asked to proceed through the flu season in its traditional manner.

Residents of the antiflu community would be asked to wear surgical masks throughout the one-month test period whenever they were outside their homes, especially when in malls and other public sites or using public transportation. If the experiment is sponsored by a governmental authority or by a private foundation or nongovernmental organization, the surgical masks might be provided free at convenient locations or sold at reduced cost through pharmacies and other outlets.

The second phase of this experiment would consist of a campaign by local governments, institutions, and businesses to disinfect doors, handles, and buttons touched frequently by large numbers of workers, customers, and others throughout working hours. Medical and public-health authorities would propose the most effective means of accomplishing this, and again, if government or nongovernmental organizations are sponsoring the overall campaign, the appropriate materials might be made available at convenient locations at no cost or reduced cost. Businesses, schools, public-transportation facilities, libraries, and other institutions would be encouraged to establish teams of personnel assigned and trained in the most effective techniques for disinfecting the surfaces that are touched frequently. Appropriate intervals for disinfecting these surfaces would be prescribed by the public health authorities.

The third phase of this experiment would consist of providing an antiseptic hand lotion to any personnel desiring it. The lotion could be provided at various locations where free dispensers could be installed—in schools, at retail stores, mass-transit facilities, and in restaurant and office restrooms.

This experiment might be conducted in Minnesota, with the Twin Cities participating in the roles of the experimental communities. Or it might be more productive to select two metropolitan areas located farther apart, in order to eliminate the cross-pollination effects that would occur through residents of one community who spend a considerable amount of their time in the adjacent community.

Although the statistics on cases of flu reported to hospitals and clinics are readily available and may be sufficient to evaluate the effectiveness of this antiflu campaign, it might be advisable to encourage any resident in the two cities who experiences unmistakable flu symptoms to provide this information to the public-health authorities.

If the antiflu city in this experiment turns out to have significantly fewer cases of flu over a typical flu season, a national plan for countering avian flu should incorporate these three procedures.

This essay was published by *The Providence Journal* several years ago. (The newspaper has granted me permission to republish it in this book.) Officers at the Naval Medical Research Center in Silver Spring, Maryland, read it and looked for a source of funding to finance an experiment similar to the one outlined in this chapter. They think that if the measures recommended in this chapter prove to reduce the number of influenza cases in the anti-flu city, plans should be made for their implementation nationwide, should an avian flu epidemic or other similar emergency arise. Some of the recommendations listed above have already been put in place by certain grocery stores and in other venues.

> YOU MUST DO THE THING YOU THINK YOU
> CANNOT DO.
>
> —ELEANOR ROOSEVELT

CHAPTER 7

A Step toward Solving the Energy Problem

The lack of consensus on a workable energy policy has driven up the cost of transportation, electricity, heating, cooling, agriculture, and manufacturing in the United States. It seems that the worse the looming economic crisis spurred by this situation appears to be, the less willing are advocates of opposing solutions to compromise and initiate any progress. This leads to deadlock and reduced productivity and could result in stagflation or recession.

With the principal contending powers unwilling to give an inch, or perhaps more appropriately a BTU, to their opponents in this heated standoff, it is time to look for measures that could possibly be satisfactory to both sides. One of these might be a new approach to the refining of petroleum.

One of the serious energy problems the United States faces is its lack of adequate petroleum-refining capacity, aggravated by reluctance of individual states to permit the construction of new refineries. It has been decades since a new oil refinery has been constructed in the United States, and consumption of refined petroleum products has increased enormously during this interval. The petroleum industry has plans for new refineries and for the expansion of some of those in existence, but there is powerful opposition to most of these projects.

Former president George W. Bush suggested that refineries be constructed on decommissioned military bases. This would help ameliorate the problem, but with so many influential residents living within sensory distance of these bases, the process of conducting environmental-impact analyses of these locations and obtaining governmental approval for their construction will take years. A partial solution to this problem might be to produce and deploy giant floating refineries built on large barges.

Such refinery barges could be moored in locations near an uninhabited or sparsely populated island, for example, where a tanker full of crude oil could tie up on one side of the refinery barge and another tanker receiving the refined product could tie up on the other. This might work well, for example, with the refinery barge moored at St. Helena in the South Atlantic. Tankers with crude oil from the Persian Gulf would moor along one side of the refinery barge, while empty tankers receiving the refined product would moor on the opposite side.

Smaller, more maneuverable tankers could be employed on the routes from St. Helena to the United States or to Europe, reducing considerably the danger of an *Exxon Valdez*-type oil spill either from grounding or collision, and making delivery of refined products to large population centers more convenient and economical.

Environmental-impact studies for these more remote refinery locations could be accomplished far more quickly than usual because of the sparse populations of human and animal life. Insurance costs for shippers and refiners would also be reduced, contributing further to the lowering of prices on the delivered product.

Deployment of these refinery barges could have important strategic benefits for the US armed services. The shipment of aviation fuel and diesel fuel to forward-deployed ships and other units would be more expeditious and less costly than it is today.

Floating refineries could help break the impasse that has come to typify energy policy in the United States.

> WHENEVER YOU ARE ASKED IF YOU CAN DO A
> JOB, TELL 'EM, "CERTAINLY I CAN!" THEN GET
> BUSY AND FIND OUT HOW TO DO IT.
> —THEODORE ROOSEVELT

CHAPTER 8

IMPROVED FUEL ECONOMY AND SAFER, LESS STRESSFUL DRIVING

A nationwide speed regulation, strictly enforced on interstate highways, could bring about far better fuel economy and less-stressful driving. The requirement would be that vehicles driven in the right lane of a two-, three-, or four-lane interstate highway would be required to drive at the posted speed limit. Several synergistic benefits will accrue from this procedure. First and foremost, there will be a significant reduction in gasoline consumption nationwide as large numbers of vehicles are driven at these lower speeds, achieving considerably better fuel economy, not only because of the more efficient engine performance but also because the drivers of vehicles in this constant-speed lane will not experience the necessity to brake and accelerate frequently, as will continue to be the case in the less-restricted lanes.

Auto accidents on interstate highways will be reduced in frequency and intensity, not only because of lower impact speeds of vehicles veering off the highway and crashing into obstructions but also because of the reduction in road-rage incidents brought about by the conflict between high-speed drivers and slower-speed drivers coming into conflict on the higher-speed lanes.

Many American citizens who would like to keep the price of gasoline from increasing and contribute in some way to reducing the trade deficit would welcome this opportunity to participate in a nationwide evolution that also gives them lower mileage costs and less stressful road trips. Even drivers with radar detectors, some of whom are obsessed with attaining the highest possible speed on every stretch of road, will welcome this new regulation; it will shift the slow-movers out of their way. Residents of sparsely populated states, who have consistently opposed speed limits of any kind, should be willing to accept this fairly benign restriction to actually make their high-speed runs in the left lane safer and less likely to be impeded than they are today.

At a time when one sector of the political spectrum's proposed solution to the oil crisis is expanded drilling, over the objection of environmentalists, and the opposing sector's solution is to impose fuel-economy restrictions on automobile manufacturers, this simple and easily implemented measure could provide at least a modicum of interim relief acceptable to all and could be put in effect immediately.

> YOU'VE GOT TO HAVE THE GUTS NOT TO BE AFRAID TO SCREW UP.
> —FUZZY ZOELLER

CHAPTER 9

A PLAN FOR FLOOD CONTROL AND FOR IMPROVING THE WORLD'S DETERIORATING WATER SUPPLY

The United Nations has announced that world water reserves are drying up fast, and booming populations, pollution, and global warming will combine to cut the average person's water supply by a third in the next twenty years. At a recent World Water Week conference, two studies were presented showing that the world's deteriorating water situation deserves more attention than ever. The reports detail how the looming water crisis is now affecting rich countries as well as poor. Global warming, diminishing wetlands, and inadequate resource management are the main causes of expanding water shortages worldwide. One-third of the human population—mostly in the developing world—is now short of water.

Here is a program that could bring a vast improvement to the quality of the world's water resources, while reducing the frequency and intensity of floods. Even though multitudes of programs dedicated to these same purposes are already in effect, and many more are being planned, this approach has at least three original features.

The first basic feature of the concept is to create, parallel to every possible waterway in the world, a pattern of holding ponds that will capture the initial overflow of each brook, creek, stream, or river following heavy rainfall or snow melt. Naturally there will be many stretches of waterways where such construction will not be practicable, but there will be hundreds of thousands of miles of waterways where this can be accomplished quite easily.

The basic design for these ponds would appear from space as a series of waffle-like indentations on both sides of the waterways wherever possible. On privately owned land, used as farm pasture, the ridges or berms around the catch basins would be no higher than approved by the landowner, probably a gradual slope of up to two or three feet; in no case would they consist of abrupt holes of any danger to livestock. In public lands not used for pasture, deeper impoundments would be possible.

With the waffle design in place along the waterways, the likelihood of a flash flood downstream will be reduced considerably, in that the initial overflow will be retained within the indentations. Even if the whole area on both sides of the waterway were to be submerged, as it might be following unusually heavy rainfall, the first two or three feet of water in the total volume will remain in the ponds, considerably lessening the force and depth of the wall of floodwater forming downstream.

Admittedly, there will be floods of such volume and force against which even the most effectively constructed waffle pond array will have little effect, but even these floods will be delayed to some extent, allowing more time for potential victims downstream to take protective or evasive action.

The second original detail in this concept is the voluntary involvement of every interested man, woman, and child in the world. Volunteer organizations ably assisted by appropriate national and local government organizations would carry out the work of constructing and maintaining these ponds. The basic unit or chapter could consist of from two to a hundred or so like-minded members dedicated to building the waffle ponds along a specific waterway allotted to them by an official or committee, probably at a local governmental level.

The concept could be developed on a trial basis in one or more member states of the United Nations. Most nations have several watersheds that experience serious floods almost every year. By concentrating considerable national and local effort on one of these watersheds for a couple of years, it should be possible to get an idea of the potential for wider application.

Once this program is explained to the population, thousands of volunteers will embrace this opportunity to make a difference in the environment. It will be easy for them to see the benefits, not only in flood prevention but in ensuring better quality water for everyone. Every cubic foot of earth they move has the potential for trapping sediment upstream from water intakes. As more and more water is trapped upstream, especially along normally dry creek beds, many new freshwater springs will emerge downstream with benefit for wildlife, livestock, and overall recreational use.

The third original element of this concept is the construction of new wetlands on tidal flats of estuarial rivers and in shallow sections of bays and sounds. Chapter 10 provides more detail on this element of the plan, including an acre-for-acre exchange for developers and farmers who would like to fill in wetlands on their properties.

This program will not solve all the world's water problems, but it is a start.

THOSE WHO CONTEMPLATE THE BEAUTY OF
THE EARTH FIND RESERVES OF STRENGTH
THAT WILL ENDURE AS LONG AS LIFE LASTS.
—RACHEL CARSON

CHAPTER 10

CREATING WETLANDS AND RECYCLING TIRES WHILE EASING PRISON OVERCROWDING

With the increasing urbanization of formerly undeveloped land and the new emphasis on corn production to serve the ethanol industry, developers and farmers are relentlessly decreasing the nation's supply of wetlands. This plan will accommodate the developers and farmers by providing them an opportunity to exchange on an acre-for-acre basis the wetlands they want to fill in for newly created wetlands in the nation's shallow estuarial rivers and bays.

The process for creating new wetlands is quite simple. Because it is labor intensive, it provides an excellent opportunity to employ nonviolent and relatively trustworthy prisoners on a voluntary basis. The prisoners would operate in a manner similar to that of the Civilian Conservation Corps in the 1930s, living in well-supervised, self-contained units near the worksites in tents, mobile homes, and on board dredge barges outfitted with living quarters. Some of the prisoners would be trained to operate a suction dredge that would be used to pump mud and sand from the river bottom into cylinders formed by lashing together layers of automobile and truck tires.

The tire arrays would be laid out in patterns that would present a sort of island in the center where the top layer of tires would be a foot or two above the water at the highest tides of the year, or in the case of inland lakes used for irrigation or for urban water supplies, above the lakes' traditional high-water marks. Surrounding this island core would be a circle of tire cylinders that would present a sort of marshland protruding from the water at low tide but slightly submerged at high tide. The outer array of tire cylinders would be laid out in patterns somewhat lower than the marshland ring, remaining submerged even at most low tides. The three different heights of the tire arrays would each support a different type of plant growth, with the submerged layer providing an environment for the growth of hydrilla and other plants native to shallow waters. This layer would subsequently become prime habitat for many of the small fish and crustaceans found at these depths.

The state or federal government entity in charge of these projects would determine the cost of creating an acre of tire-cylinder marshland and would allow developers and farmers to fill in an equivalent acreage at a location of their choice after paying the determined fee. Most of the newly created marshland developed under this program would be of greater benefit to the environment than the wetlands filled in by developers and farmers.

The constant filtering of river, estuary, or bay water down through the marshland sections of the tire islands at each ebb tide would remove many of the pollutants and collect debris floating in the water. These islands would increase in size year after year as they collect logs, silt, and other materials that will wash over them during floods. By being filled with dredge spoil, the tire cylinders as well as the spaces between them will have greater stability against erosion than would islands of similar size but without the inner structure. The tires and plastic or nylon straps that would be used to attach them together are virtually indestructible, contributing to the islands' permanence.

The areas of the river, estuary, and bay bottoms from which the spoil is dredged will also help improve water quality. The holes, trenches, and channels left by the dredging will slow the currents passing over them, allowing still more silt to settle out. In some parts of the waterways being dredged, arrangements can be made with landowners on adjacent shores to have the dredging process create channels to their boat slips, allowing them to operate deeper-draft boats than would have been possible previously. This would be another source of income to help support the overall effort.

I think there will be plenty of volunteers from the state and federal prisons to man a large number of these projects. Even though the work will be strenuous and dirty, if the men are provided adequate bathing facilities, clean living quarters, and good food, they will prefer this way of serving out their sentences to the more stultifying existence they experience behind prison walls. Prisoners who are particularly good workers could be given reductions in sentences and other benefits.

Since this work will open up dredging in many areas where it is not currently conducted, it will not displace commercial dredging operations. In fact, some commercial dredgers will find work training the prisoners and perhaps will provide supervisory personnel.

There will be many concomitant benefits from these projects, most of which will contribute to the nation's economy. Tourism, hunting, and fishing opportunities will be enhanced in the vicinity of these projects. The cost of disposing of large quantities of used tires will be vastly reduced, and thousands of acres of marginally valuable wetlands will be made available for urban and industrial development and for agriculture, increasing the tax base of the regions affected.

> I CANNOT ENDURE TO WASTE ANYTHING AS
> PRECIOUS AS AUTUMN SUNSHINE BY STAYING
> IN THE HOUSE. SO I SPEND ALMOST ALL THE
> DAYLIGHT HOURS IN THE OPEN AIR.
> —NATHANIEL HAWTHORNE

CHAPTER 11

COUNTERING FOREST AND BRUSH FIRES WHILE EASING PRISON OVERCROWDING

With the current problems several states are experiencing with forest fires and brush fires, I have developed a plan similar to the one described in chapter 10, but directed at removing the undergrowth in the nation's forests and the small trees and bushes that burn the mountainsides of several states every year. This plan will also help ameliorate two other problems that are costing the nation millions of dollars each year. The three problems that will be solved are

1. brush fires and forest fires,
2. pollution from coal-fired power plants, and
3. prison overcrowding.

My plan is to form groups of nonviolent prisoners, who can be trusted to work outside the prison, into teams that remove brush from areas prone to frequent brush fires and undergrowth from forests that are deemed by Forest Service officials to be susceptible to forest fires.

The teams of prisoners would operate in a manner similar to that implemented by the Civilian Conservation Corps in the 1930s. They would live in tents or mobile homes, moving from location to location as they cleared brush and forest areas. They would be self-contained units, the cooks and logistic-support personnel selected primarily from the prisoners themselves, but with supervisory officials present.

The bushes and underbrush that they remove will be fed into shredders. The shredded material will be loaded into trucks and hauled to the closest coal-fired power plant, where it will be mixed with the coal supply. Since there are fewer pollutants such as sulfur and mercury in the wood chips, these power plants would benefit not only from the free source of fuel but from reduced toxicity in their emissions.

If at some time in the future, science comes up with a process for converting these wood chips into ethanol or other automotive fuel, some of this material could be diverted to this use.

Although the work the prisoners would accomplish would be tedious, dirty, and uncomfortable, if they are given adequate bathing facilities, good food and laundry services, and clean living quarters in their camps, most of them would prefer this lifestyle to the more regimented and stultifying existence in the walled prisons.

There should be no outcry from labor unions that their members are being forced out of traditional jobs, and the Teamsters Union would be quite supportive of the program, in that their members would probably be driving the trucks from the shredding sites to the power plants.

Organizations that are looking for causes to criticize the government on behalf of supposedly abused workers will probably accuse the government of utilizing slave labor. To counter this possibility, it would be advisable to use only prisoners who volunteer for this project as team members. Prisoners whose supervisors rate as superior performers could be given reduced sentences and other incentives after appropriate periods of participation.

This is a win-win-win solution to the problems of brush and forest fires, power-plant pollution, and prison overcrowding.

A variation on this theme might be accomplished with the cooperation of the Chinese government. Thousands of empty containers are returned to Chinese seaports every week. These containers could be filled with wood chips that could be mixed with the coal fed into coal-fired power plants in China, contributing to a much-needed amelioration of power-plant pollution there.

This would be particularly valuable to the Chinese in the near future as they try to improve the quality of their air. Chinese workers could even be offered jobs clearing the brush and undergrowth in the United States, with the offer of residence and citizenship following an appropriate period of work. Since there is a significant problem with illegal Chinese immigration, this would provide a legitimate alternative to these prospective immigrants, as well as a more controlled and documented workforce.

Another aspect of this project could be the conversion of much of the timber and brush removed from the described swaths into charcoal. Several nations are large importers of charcoal, making this a potentially profitable enterprise.

> LIVE AS IF YOU ARE ONE WITH THE TREES, THE RIVERS, THE MOUNTAINS AND THE WHOLE UNIVERSE WILL EMBRACE YOU LIKE A FRIEND.
> —CITATION FROM HOLY VEDAS

CHAPTER 12

AIRBORNE ASSETS COULD ASSIST IN COUNTERING ILLEGAL IMMIGRATION

Illegal immigration across the Mexican and Canadian borders could be reduced significantly while providing valuable training for US Air Force, Navy, and Coast Guard air crews (especially Air National Guard and Naval Air Reserve squadrons) employing several new airborne sensors while coordinating operations with forces on the ground.

The idea would be to conduct well-coordinated patrols, both day and night, along the US borders with Mexico and Canada by both manned and unmanned aircraft employing state-of-the-art radar and advanced infrared (IR) and optical sensors capable of detecting infiltrators. Voice communications with appropriate forces on the ground would provide the border patrol and other law-enforcement organizations real-time information on the location of infiltrators. The aircraft could operate out of air force bases and naval air stations adjacent to the border areas. Canadian aircraft might also participate in the campaign.

During the war in Vietnam, similar reconnaissance of Route 1, the coastal highway of North Vietnam, was conducted at night by marine F-3D aircraft equipped with primitive side-looking infrared sensors and later by RA-5C reconnaissance aircraft. The missions were revealing, showing vehicular traffic, but the IR data were not real time, so they were of little use in carrying out immediate action. But now, with better communications between air and ground forces and with aircraft equipped with much-improved sensors, these tactics would be operationally effective. The advanced radar would be particularly effective, in that it would provide all-weather detection of illegal immigrants.

In addition to providing infiltration information to ground forces, some of the reconnoitering aircraft, or perhaps Homeland Security-contracted crop-duster type aircraft vectored to the infiltration scene by the military aircraft, could be equipped with tanks capable of dispensing a cloud of nontoxic but hard-to-remove paint or mist on the infiltrators, similar to that used to explode on bank robbers escaping with specially prepared money bags.

The infiltrators would be easily identified for several days following their interception and would be apprehended with far less uncertainty than is currently the case with suspected illegal immigrants. These tactics would provide excellent training for aircrews and would be far more effective than the currently employed ground patrols and fences. A concomitant benefit could be obtained by deploying units of air and ground forces that would later work together carrying out similar assignments along the borders of Afghanistan.

This program would also have a synergistic effect related to the concept of reducing global warming described in chapter 1. The hard-to-remove but nontoxic paint would remain on the ground, especially in rocky and desert areas, reflecting the sun's rays back into space. In fact, if an excuse is needed to dispense this paint over border areas, the global warming motive could be presented as the primary purpose. If by coincidence the paint just happened to fall on an illegal immigrant, it would just be a fortuitous secondary benefit.

ACTION MAY NOT ALWAYS BRING HAPPINESS, BUT THERE IS NO HAPPINESS WITHOUT ACTION.

—BENJAMIN DISRAELI

CHAPTER 13

RESTORATION BASKETBALL

Once upon a time, basketball could be played and enjoyed by men and women of all heights. But over the past half century, it has become a sport dominated by players nearly seven feet tall. Although three-point shooters of shorter stature still have their moments, most of the scoring is done by giants skilled at muscling their way through defenders to simply slam the ball down into the net while hanging on the rim. This form of basketball will always have a multitude of fans, especially in the professional arenas, but there may be a way to bring this sport back to the days when anyone could play.

The new version would be played under the same rules as the current game, with one exception: all shots would have to be made from outside a semicircular zone twelve feet from the basket. Players would be allowed inside this zone with or without the ball, but only players whose feet are either planted outside the zone or who leave the floor from outside the zone and release the ball before landing inside the zone will be eligible to score. No layups, tip-ins or alley-oops will be allowed. Players recovering rebounds will have to pass or dribble the ball outside the zone before the next shot is made. Any player with even one foot on the floor inside this zone as the shot is made or whose jump shot results from a foot leaving the floor from inside the zone will have created an automatic turnover to the opposing team.

This new form of the game will be very popular at high schools and at smaller colleges where the teams are not essentially farm teams for the NBA.

Talented athletes of all heights will be able to participate. Although games played under the new rules will be lower scoring, the playmaking and shooting skills displayed will restore the excitement that once electrified the arena. It is unlikely that this version of the game will replace the current game at the professional or college level, but I can see it becoming part of a doubleheader performance at high school games, where the restoration basketball teams would play a preliminary game in place of the more traditional second team or junior high team games, as is the case today in many schools.

Restoration basketball will also be popular on neighborhood courts, where it will bring out hundreds of young players previously discouraged from participating because of their lack of height. Restoration basketball will also be a considerably faster game than today's version, in that there will be far fewer fouls called. The majority of the fouls committed today are inflicted on players making their shots from within twelve feet of the basket. Giant players will still be of great value, especially in defending and rebounding, but quick, talented players of all heights will once more have an opportunity to shine.

> YOU GROW UP THE DAY YOU HAVE YOUR FIRST
> REAL LAUGH AT YOURSELF.
> —ETHEL BARRYMORE

CHAPTER 14

AEROSPACERS: AN ORGANIZATION TO IMPROVE TRAINING IN SCIENCE AND TECHNOLOGY

From recent surveys of American grade school and high school levels of achievement, it is clear that in general, American schools are not turning out students as well prepared academically as several foreign school systems are or as well prepared as previous generations in the United States were. This is particularly evident in the areas of mathematics and physics and is having a deleterious effect on the qualifications of young people entering the technical workforce.

A program to improve this situation could be sponsored by the defense industry, the military services, and the National Aeronautics and Space Administration (NASA), all of which would benefit from a process wherein an elite group of young men and women could be placed on a track very early in their academic years that would lead them to careers in science, industry, and defense.

Organizations such as the Aerospace Industries Association (AIA) and the National Defense Industrial Association (NDIA) might add such participation to smaller-scale educational programs already in place.

The basic idea would be to create a national and perhaps even an international organization similar to the Boy Scouts of America, but with the emphasis on becoming prepared for careers in national defense rather than on outdoor survival. It might be called Aerospacers. The members achieving qualification in defense knowledge and capability—similar to the level of attainment of an Eagle Scout—would provide a constantly renewable source of astronauts, aviators, engineers, analysts, and technicians. Even those who participate in the program but may not be sufficiently qualified, interested, or motivated to attain the highest achievement would still contribute to a better-informed and supportive citizenry.

Any attempt to incorporate the public-school system in this program to develop young careers in national defense would most likely run into barriers and resistance from administrators and others that would defeat its purpose, so I would recommend that it be administered outside the formal education structure.

My idea would be for the military organizations, perhaps in conjunction with NASA and the military services, to develop courses of study that individual Aerospacers could pursue on their own, primarily via the Internet. I don't think it would be advisable to try to organize the Aerospacers into units such as cub packs and scout troops with regular meetings, because the success of this type of structure is so heavily dependent on the qualification and motivation of the adult leadership.

I think periodic gatherings of Aerospacers from the same geographical area to participate in examinations qualifying them for the next progressive step in their careers would be a better arrangement, because these meetings could be organized and carried out by NDIA, AIA, NASA, or military personnel with proper qualifications.

An important feature of this concept would be the opportunity for the most highly qualified Aerospacers to serve as summer interns at NASA, military facilities, and in the defense industries, where they would be given responsibilities commensurate with their abilities and where they would meet with successful role models.

I would guess that many of these young men and women would be accepted later in the military academies and in high-quality civilian schools where aerospace- and defense-related courses and degrees are available. Once the Aerospacers have graduated from college and are active in NASA, the military services, and in the defense industry, they would become the mentors and role models for the younger Aerospacers.

By continuing their membership as Aerospacers throughout their careers, they would forge and maintain bonds of friendship and camaraderie that will bring together personnel of quite diverse occupations but with the common interest in aerospace.

> WE CANNOT ALWAYS BUILD THE FUTURE FOR OUR YOUTH, BUT WE CAN BUILD OUR YOUTH FOR THE FUTURE.
> —FRANKLIN D. ROOSEVELT

CHAPTER 15

COMBINED STADIUM, HOTEL, AND CONVENTION CENTERS

The solution to the problem of financing new football, baseball, and soccer stadia is to encourage the team's owners, the host city, and a hotel company to build a stadium that is a multipurpose hotel, convention center, and entertainment venue. Such a design would have synergistic features that would make it a profitable entity rather than a burden on the city's taxpayers and businesses.

Instead of the luxurious boxes for privileged fans in traditional style, I would provide a ring of hotel rooms facing the ball field. These rooms would have balconies from which the games could be observed comfortably. Occupancy for these rooms would be auctioned off to the highest bidder for game days.

Immediately behind the wall separating the seating areas and the ring of hotel rooms facing the field would be a large section of indoor parking. Parking spaces adjacent to the hotel rooms would be reserved for the rooms' occupants. The parking garage would insulate convention halls, restaurants, and other businesses from the noise of games, concerts, or other events underway on the field.

The exterior of the stadium would consist of hotel rooms, most of which would feature picturesque views of the surrounding neighborhood.

If the stadium is primarily for baseball, the stadium seats from home plate out beyond first and third base would be covered by a roof that could also be extended mechanically to cover the infield as far from home plate as the pitcher's mound. A flexible curtain could be lowered from the movable roof all the way to the ground, providing a convention hall-like amphitheater suitable for concerts and similar events.

The structure would include smaller convention halls and meeting rooms, restaurants, shops, and indoor parking. At least one of the restaurants should feature an outdoor terrace overlooking the best available exterior view.

In order to make it more convenient for hotel guests to reach the rooms that do not have adjacent parking spaces, there should be reception desks at opposite ends of the building, with moving walkways on the ground floor and elevators and escalators located strategically.

This facility would be of economic benefit to its owners, the host city, local businesses, and visitors to the city. It could very well become the most popular venue in the area, providing essential and entertaining services seven days a week. Unlike the conventional football or baseball stadium, the extensive parking area, both indoor and outdoor, would be in use on a daily basis, rather than only on game days.

> AS LONG AS YOU'RE GOING TO BE THINKING ANYWAY, THINK BIG.
>
> —DONALD TRUMP

CHAPTER 16

A REVOLUTION IN TELEVISION PROGRAMMING AND ADVERTISING

I have been concerned over the years by the wasteland so extensively inhabited by American television viewers. Currently the commercial television channels pander programming to what the majority of viewers between the ages of eighteen and twenty-eight prefer, and even the twenty-four-hour cable news channels attempt to outdo each other in presenting shouting or otherwise contentious spokesmen, who tend to be carnival barkers rather than authentic commentators.

The following concept would provide a financial incentive for viewers to tune in to commercials on the hour and half hour on an educational or other culture-enhancing channel. My idea is to lure even the hoi polloi away from the commercials on their wrestling, reality, or sitcom channels on the hour and half hour. They will be invited to trade their attention for a possible monetary reward on a more philanthropic or educational channel that would have relatively low programming costs and therefore could afford to reward its viewers with a fairly large share of the money paid by advertisers.

I think that the market for commercials on this channel would increase substantially and cumulatively as more and more viewers became aware of the possible rewards. This channel could therefore charge increasingly larger fees to its advertisers and at the same time award more and larger prizes to the viewers.

This plan has the potential for revolutionizing television programming and advertising while simultaneously improving the quality of the former and reducing the cost of the latter. A concomitant benefit, that will be especially welcome at this point in the nation's economic cycle, will be an infusion of cash into the hands of the people most inclined to spend it, hence an improvement in consumer spending and consumer confidence. Because television advertising costs may come down after this plan is implemented, the cost of financing political campaigns might also be reduced, making it less likely that only the candidates with massive financial resources can be elected.

The basic principle of this concept is to motivate the television audience to switch to an educational or other type of culture-enhancing channel (henceforth called Channel 1) from whatever channel they are watching, at the commercial breaks on the hour and half hour. Then, as soon as the commercial break is over, Channel 1 representatives would place hundreds of telephone calls all over the country (and abroad wherever Channel 1 is available) using the following format.

"Good evening. I'm calling from Channel 1. If you can identify the products just advertised on Channel 1, I am prepared to send you a check for one hundred dollars." If the responder answers correctly, the representative will continue, "Good. Your check will be in the mail tomorrow. If you have the time to answer a few additional questions, I'll send you an additional reward." The representative would then ask one or two questions about the commercials and the products, such as: "Do you currently drive a Buick? Did the commercial you have just seen make it more likely that you might consider buying a Buick?" These questions would be provided by the advertisers, and the responses would give them some feedback on the effectiveness of the specific commercial. For answering the questions, the responder would be given an additional cash reward or a coupon or some other appropriate gift selected by the advertiser.

If the responder replies that he or she isn't able to name the products just advertised, the Channel 1 representative will say, "If you would like to receive queries like this one from Channel 1, I will place your phone number in a pool for random selection for future calls, and if you will answer two additional questions, I'll mail you a check for ten dollars." If the answer is yes, the representative will ask, "Were you viewing a television channel when I called you, and if so, can you identify the channel?" If the answer is yes, the representative will continue, "Can you remember what products were advertised on the last commercial break?" The data acquired from these brief interviews would be compiled in a report that I believe would be more valuable to television advertisers than the data provided by Nielsen and other television surveys and would provide the Channel 1 organization a significant additional source of revenue.

The philanthropic aspect of this concept could take the form of one or more of the following program formats.

1. Channel 1 would be an educational channel, providing formal, high-quality instruction, much in the manner that certain community colleges are currently doing. This could be done as a collaborative effort with any educational institutions interested in participating. In effect, the lecture portion of the curriculum would occur on Channel 1, with student participation occurring at sites designated by the participating institutions.

2. Channel 1 would be a cultural channel, presenting live and previously recorded high-quality musical and dramatic events produced by the smaller cities that currently get little national exposure. Some universities produce concerts, operas, plays, and musicals of high enough quality to be telecast under this format.

3. Channel 1 would be a forum for discussion of serious national issues. Political parties and other organizations would be offered the opportunity to provide their best-qualified debaters to engage in formal debates moderated by Channel 1 hosts.

4. Channel 1 would be a combination of the above-listed formats, perhaps with the educational segments running during the day and late at night and the cultural and public-affairs segments running at prime time. The occasional inclusion of athletic events might also be a feature of the combined format. These could be athletic events not covered by the networks, such as Ivy League and small-town/small-college baseball, football, and basketball.

In effect, Channel 1 has the potential for transferring some of the money currently being paid to performers, producers, and marketers, to the viewing public, the people who really deserve to be rewarded by the advertisers for watching their commercials.

In order to compete with Channel 1, the major networks and other channels would probably imitate the cash-reward technique for holding or luring viewers, but since their programming costs are much higher, they couldn't offer as valuable and as many rewards as would be the case with Channel 1. This would force them to pay less for programming and quite possibly lessen the severity and attractiveness of sensationalism. As more and more of the advertising revenue ends up in the hands of the viewers rather than the performers, producers, and others, a more reasonable system of compensation for the currently overpaid athletes, sitcom stars, and anchorpersons would evolve, and overall advertising costs would probably decrease. At any rate, Channel 1 could eventually become the dominant television advertising venue and would find it relatively easy to maintain this dominance.

If one of the nation's philanthropic foundations would implement this concept, it could bring about the most beneficial change in American culture and politics since the invention of the Internet.

FREEDOM IS THE RIGHT TO TELL PEOPLE
WHAT THEY DO NOT WANT TO HEAR.
—GEORGE ORWELL

CHAPTER 17

THE INTERSTATE HIGHWAY GUIDE

These publications might be titled *Pennsylvania Interstate* or *Florida Interstate*—whatever state it is being distributed in. It would contain as its centerfold a large, good-quality map of the particular state, with hundreds of keyed symbols found easily from grid coordinates spelled out in various categorical listings. The categorical listings, appearing on other pages of the publication, would show hotels, motels, service stations, hospitals, parks, locations of special events, and so forth.

An important feature of this publication would take the form of rebates offered by advertisers, whereby the person in possession of a particular issue would present his copy to the advertisers, who would then provide the discounted product. Feature stories describing local attractions and historic sites, again keyed to the centerfold map, would provide tourists and others passing through the state with a convenient and useful guide to areas of interest. In this respect it would duplicate some of the information currently provided by the American Automobile Association and similar organizations but at considerably less cost.

Travelers with specific preferences for motels, restaurants, theme parks, and service stations would find these guides extremely useful in planning each day's travel timing and itinerary.

Although the principal return on investment to the company that produces these guides would come from the advertisers, the guide could be sold at service stations, hotels, restaurants, and magazine stands for an appropriate price.

The guides could be published on a monthly, quarterly, semiannual, or annual basis, depending on the level of activity in the individual states and the market for advertising.

A variation on this theme would be to involve a company such as Google or Yahoo in producing these guides. That way the guides could be made available electronically as well as in printed form. A traveler planning a trip through several states could download the guides for the targeted states and consult them as necessary on a laptop or tablet. The electronic versions could be kept up to date on a daily, even hourly basis, with advice on road conditions, detours, and developing special events.

> THE TOUGHEST THING ABOUT SUCCESS IS THAT YOU'VE GOT TO KEEP ON BEING A SUCCESS.
>
> —IRVING BERLIN

CHAPTER 18

FOOT-TREADLE ELECTRIC GENERATORS AS ACCESSORIES FOR COMPUTERS

With worldwide concern over the need to find alternate sources of energy, I think a small but significant contribution could be made through the use of foot-treadle-operated electric generators as accessories to computers. A campaign to implement this project would have five distinct advantages.

1. It will reduce consumption of externally supplied electricity in all buildings where it is implemented and ultimately pay for itself through reduced electricity costs.
2. It will enable office workers to operate their computers and other electrically powered equipment during extended power outages.
3. It will contribute to the health and fitness of the workforce.
4. It will have a beneficial effect on several sectors of the US manufacturing industry.
5. Once implemented by a federal or state agency or a large business organization, it will motivate and encourage others to emulate the example in businesses, institutions, and homes throughout the nation.

The procedure would be to provide any worker who is willing to participate in the program a small electric generator operated by a foot treadle similar to those used in sewing machines before the availability of electrically powered sewing machines. The generator would be connected to the worker's computer battery. The program could be initiated as follows.

Step 1. The government agency or other large organization would issue a request for proposals to American manufacturers to develop and produce a treadle-type generator suitable for installation in office venues.

Step 2. The government agency or business organization would find out how many of its personnel would be willing, on a voluntary basis, to use one of these generators to charge the batteries of their computers.

Step 3. The government agency or business organization would select and fund the three best proposals for the generators and buy and distribute the number of generators indicated in step 2.

Step 4. The government agency or business organization would provide information as to cost savings, workforce health, and emergency responsiveness to other government agencies and business organizations, encouraging them to participate in the treadle-generator project, thus bringing down the cost of the generators and reducing electricity consumption.

This program will pay for itself in reduced electricity costs, result in a healthier federal workforce, and provide for continuous communication capabilities during emergencies resulting in power outages.

IT IS A COMMON EXPERIENCE THAT A PROBLEM DIFFICULT AT NIGHT IS RESOLVED IN THE MORNING AFTER THE COMMITTEE OF SLEEP HAS WORKED ON IT.

—JOHN STEINBECK

CHAPTER 19

A NEW POLITICAL PARTY CAPABLE OF WINNING ELECTIONS WITH REDUCED CAMPAIGN FINANCING

Although the nation's two principal political parties have millions of members who have the nation's best interests at heart, these voters are generally outmaneuvered at the primary election by the parties' most doctrinaire elements. In the case of the Republican Party, the extreme right wing would include voters opposed to abortion, gay marriage, inheritance taxes, organized labor, government regulation, government-funded medical care, gun control of any kind, and the teaching of evolution. In the case of the Democratic Party, the voters of the extreme left would find it difficult to vote for any candidate who did not support the positions outlined above as anathema to Republicans. In addition, the left-wing Democrats would support higher taxes on the wealthy and corporations and severe reductions in the emission of greenhouse gases, restrictions on industrial development, and a multitude of other issues of environmental protectionism.

Since these two extreme wings of their respective parties are "true believers" and more likely to participate in primary elections than their more moderate brethren, neither party is apt to produce a moderate candidate for national office, thus eliminating from contention the moderate candidates who are more likely to act in the nation's best interest rather than in accordance with a strict doctrine defined by the parties' extremists. Some third parties manage to pull enough votes from one or the other dominant parties to influence an election, as was the case with Ralph Nader in 2000, helping to elect George W. Bush, even though most of Nader's followers supported far more of the positions on major issues favored by Al Gore.

Independent voters are primarily moderates and not so dedicated to the ideological positions held by the two major parties as to prevent them from voting for whom they think is the least undesirable candidate, regardless of party affiliation.

Once the major parties have selected their candidates for national office, their strategists soften some of their positions on the more polarizing issues in order to attract independents as well as more moderate members of the opposing party. The best example of this was the ability of Ronald Reagan's team to lure to his side the "Reagan Democrats."

Television has become the most important political venue, and as a result, enormous amounts of money are required to elect a candidate, not only to try to persuade the independents and susceptible moderates, but to keep the party faithful whipped into a frenzy of hate for their opponents and into a patriotic fervor strong enough to get them to the polls. Both parties become beholden to large campaign contributors in order to accumulate the funds required for increasingly expensive television commercials, so no matter which party wins, the election lobbyists who can point to their organization's contributions will have a hand in writing the laws that affect their various businesses.

I am proposing the establishment of a new political party, dedicated to the national interest rather than to parochial interests. It will take several years to develop this party, so at the outset I recommend that moderate Republicans and moderate Democrats who might be interested in the new party remain in their respective parties until such time as the new party is capable of electing a member to the US Congress in their respective districts. It is unlikely that many members of the "true believer" wings of the Republican and Democratic parties will join the new party, in that its primary purpose will be to govern in the national interest rather than in the interests of specific ideological groups, lobbyists, and campaign contributors.

I am suggesting the new political party be called the Century Party and its members called Centurions. The party's basic unit would include up to ten members. These units would meet once a month, preferably on the same day as all the other units, so that the results of the meetings could be forwarded electronically up the party structure on that day. Each unit will elect a leader who will designate the monthly meeting location and will assign responsibilities to the members.

At each meeting all the units throughout the nation will discuss one issue that has been announced at the previous meeting. The issue will be one that is deemed by the Century Party leadership to be one of the most important facing the nation at the moment. The unit leaders will assign one member to make a case for each of the principal solutions being proposed by spokesmen of national stature. After both, or in some cases multiple, positions on the issue have been presented by the assigned supporter, the unit membership will discuss the issue, and following the discussion, a vote will be taken. The unit leader will forward the results to the party leadership, who will compile the results and then recommend to the entire party membership to support this position in letters to congressmen and senators.

Once each quarter, the leaders of the ten units located in close proximity will meet. This meeting will be a starting place for preparing personnel to run for political office. If one or more of the unit leaders is interested in running for United States Congress, for example, he or she will be given an opportunity to explain to the other nine leaders why he or she should be supported. Whether or not one of these ten leaders wants to run for office, this group of ten will elect one of its number to represent their one hundred Centurions at a semiannual meeting attended by all the leaders of hundred-Centurion groups in the congressional district. At this semiannual meeting, the group leaders will hear from each of the group leaders who would like to represent the party at the next election. Following the presentations by all who would like to run, nominating presentations will be made by other attendees, followed by a vote.

If the leadership considers that there are enough Centurions in the congressional district to elect a congressman, all the Centurions in the district will be asked to make a small contribution in order to pay for the basic costs of the campaign. It is not expected that these costs will be significant, in that no Centurion will be nominated until the party membership in the district is numerous enough to elect its nominee. As more and more nonmembers of the party become aware of the party and its dedication to the national interest rather than to parochial interests, many of these voters, primarily independents, will vote for the Centurion candidate rather than for less-principled candidates from the Democratic and Republican parties.

Once the party has adequate membership to elect a senator, the same process used to develop congressional candidates will be implemented on a statewide basis, with all the leaders of hundred-Centurion groups attending a convention to select the statewide nominee. Eventually, when the party has enough members to elect a president, a similar national convention will be held.

For several years moderate Democrats and Republicans will maintain dual-party membership, but once the Century Party is numerous enough to elect an official, its dual-party members will be asked to abandon the old party membership.

Since there are far more moderate Democrats, Republicans, and independents than there are extreme right-wing Republicans or extreme left-wing Democrats, the Century Party will eventually become the majority party for the rest of the century.

The two traditional parties will continue to elect some congressmen and even a senator or two, but the Century Party will lead the nation to a far more successful future than could result from a continuation of the current hopeless mess.

> I HAVE COME TO THE CONCLUSION THAT POLITICS ARE TOO SERIOUS A MATTER TO BE LEFT TO THE POLITICIANS.
> —CHARLES DE GAULLE

CHAPTER 20

IMPROVING DOWNTOWN TRAFFIC

This concept promotes the construction of overpasses over busy downtown intersections that are currently significant traffic bottlenecks. In a typical installation, the overpass would carry the north-south traffic above the east-west traffic which would remain as it is, only without traffic signals. A cost/benefit study would be conducted prior to construction to calculate the cost in passenger time lost currently by motorists waiting for the signal to change, as well as the cost of fuel wasted while the vehicles sit idling at the light, carbon dioxide expelled by these vehicles, and so on.

These installations should be constructed at alternating intersections so that drivers wishing to make a turn would have that opportunity at every other intersection like one-way streets now. Concomitant benefits would be the creation of additional downtown commercial space underneath the ramp areas. In cities located in areas where earthquakes occur, the space beneath the overpasses would provide shelter for vehicles and pedestrians where they could be protected from collapsing buildings in the vicinity.

> THE TROUBLE WITH LIFE ISN'T THAT THERE IS
> NO ANSWER, IT'S THAT THERE ARE SO MANY
> ANSWERS.
>
> —RUTH BENEDICT

CHAPTER 21

A VOLUNTEER ORGANIZATION TO ASSIST IN HOMELAND SECURITY

Many American citizens would like to contribute to homeland security in ways other than paying the taxes that finance the activities of the Department of Homeland Security. These citizens could participate in ways that would assist the department in protecting the nation from terrorists attempting to kill Americans and to destroy buildings, monuments, and infrastructure. In order to enable these citizens to become involved in such a campaign, something along the order of the Civil Defense organization of World War II vintage should be organized.

The Department of Homeland Security is already working with volunteer groups in several cities and states, primarily in the areas of assisting the populace to recover from a terrorist attack. That work should continue and should be expanded to include every city and state. But even more valuable would be an organization to help prevent terrorist attacks. Whereas in the World War II Civil Defense organization, air-raid wardens patrolled the streets, making sure all lights were out during blackouts, similar wardens would now observe the approaches to high-value targets, with priority given to those identified by the FBI or other agencies as high on the terrorist list of objectives. These would include major bridges, nuclear-power plants, toxic-chemical storage, and so forth.

In some cases, where large numbers of volunteers are available, for example around the Golden Gate (San Francisco) or the Verrazano Narrows (New York City) bridges, the observers might be provided observation posts from where they could scan assigned sectors, watching out for activities deemed by the Homeland Security experts to be typical of terrorist preparations for an attack. They should be equipped with night-vision binoculars and cell phones. In more remote areas, for example a nuclear-power plant or natural-gas pipeline substation, one or more television cameras could be erected to provide coverage of access routes and other vulnerability sectors. Volunteers located in meeting rooms of civic organizations, in veterans' organizations, for example, could be assigned the responsibility for monitoring these sites via television screens and would report any unusual activity to appropriate authorities.

Although very large numbers of volunteers could be expected to participate in this program, it should not be a very expensive plan to implement. With the exception of night-vision devices, most of the equipment required could be provided by the volunteers themselves—for example, binoculars, telescopes, flashlights, and cell phones. Surveillance television cameras should be provided by the Department of Homeland Security, as well as inexpensive armbands and headgear identifying the designated volunteers as trained and certified participants.

In addition to providing considerably more awareness of the environment around potential terrorist targets, the very presence of the volunteers would serve as somewhat of a deterrent to potential terrorists, perhaps causing them to shift their objectives from these high-value targets to something less important.

Thousands of Americans would gladly contribute their time to this endeavor, relieving their current feeling of helplessness in the face of very real threats. It would be difficult to devise a more cost-effective program than this one to enhance homeland security.

> WHEN ONE DOOR CLOSES, ANOTHER OPENS;
> BUT WE OFTEN LOOK SO LONG AND SO
> REGRETFULLY UPON THE CLOSED DOOR THAT
> WE DO NOT SEE THE ONE WHICH HAS OPENED.
> —ALEXANDER GRAHAM BELL

CHAPTER 22

REVITALIZING AMERICA'S LARGE CITIES WHILE REDUCING TRAFFIC CONGESTION AND IMPROVING THE ENVIRONMENT

One of the principal causes of traffic congestion and its deleterious impact on energy consumption, pollution, and environmental degradation in large cities is the shortage of housing in the vicinity of commercial buildings. A steady amelioration of this condition could be achieved simply by city governments requiring new commercial construction to include either within the new building or within six blocks of the building, sufficient residential housing for at least 20 percent of the workforce anticipated to occupy the new building.

Additional downtown housing could be developed by requiring the owners of currently constructed commercial buildings to either modify the building to incorporate housing for at least 20 percent of the occupants or to construct equivalent housing within six blocks of the commercial building. The schedule for modifying these buildings or for requiring housing construction within six blocks of the building could be based on the age of the building. For example, the owners of buildings over forty years old could be required to comply with the new-construction formula within the next five years. Owners of buildings thirty-nine years old would be required to complete the new construction formula within the next six years.

This same process would be carried out by including a new year-group annually until all the commercial buildings in the city have either been modified to include housing for 20 percent of the workforce or the owners have constructed an equivalent amount of residential housing within six blocks of the commercial building. The owners of the buildings could provide either apartments or condominium-type units, the only requirement being that at least 20 percent of the workforce would be accommodated by the residential units. There should be no restriction as to the size or luxuriousness of the residential units, but there would be some incentive to provide relatively affordable housing in that the 20 percent requirement could be met more economically if at least some of the new units are relatively small.

In addition to the reductions in traffic congestion and energy consumption to be derived from this concept, there will be many concomitant benefits, including the revitalization of the commercial centers of large cities, with restaurants and other establishments previously dedicated primarily to lunch-hour business staying open for dinner and other evening activities. Because of this increased population presence, inner-city crime rates would decrease.

An even more important contribution to the future of the cities brought about by the implementation of this concept will be the income tax, sales tax, and other revenue increases that will accrue to the city because of the eventual population shift from suburbs to city center. Suburban communities and counties will also benefit from this program, in that the demands for new highways, streets, water, sewer, electricity, and other infrastructure will be reduced as more residents in the overall area choose to live in the newly available accommodations in the city, where the infrastructure already exists.

ONE OF THE ADVANTAGES OF BEING
DISORDERLY IS THAT ONE IS CONSTANTLY
MAKING EXCITING DISCOVERIES.
—A. A. MILNE

CHAPTER 23

PRESERVING THE NATION'S DEFICIENT BRIDGES UNTIL SUCH TIME AS THEY CAN BE REPAIRED OR REPLACED

A relatively simple and inexpensive procedure can allow the nation's deficient bridges to remain safely in use until such time as they can be repaired or replaced. Since the bridges' vulnerabilities are heavily influenced by the number of vehicles on their surfaces at any given time, structural engineers can calculate the maximum number of vehicles each of these deficient bridges can accommodate at one time without causing additional weakening of the structure. Then the bridges can have cross-hatched sections painted on the surfaces to indicate the minimum distance between vehicles that will be allowed on that specific bridge. A vehicle approaching one of the crosshatched sections would be obliged to slow down enough to permit the preceding vehicle to exit the crosshatched section before entering it.

Even though this procedure may cause traffic backups during rush hours, it will allow traffic to flow uninterruptedly and if strictly enforced will extend the bridges' useful lifespans until they can be repaired or replaced. It may be the only effective procedure that could be implemented without delay, and it would be a very positive step in reducing the anxiety that the driving public has developed since the collapse of the Minneapolis bridge not long ago and the subsequent report on potentially unsafe bridges.

> IN ANY MOMENT OF DECISION THE BEST THING YOU CAN DO IS THE RIGHT THING, THE NEXT BEST THING IS THE WRONG THING, AND THE WORST THING YOU CAN DO IS NOTHING.
>
> —THEODORE ROOSEVELT

CHAPTER 24

EARTHQUAKE-RESISTANT BUILDINGS UTILIZING THE AIR RIGHTS ABOVE DOWNTOWN INTERSECTIONS

This idea could be very valuable if implemented in Californian and Japanese city centers and other metropolitan areas vulnerable to earthquakes. The basic concept is to develop the air rights over certain downtown intersections. Structures designed with the most modern earthquake-resistant features would be built over some of the larger intersections in the cities, providing additional commercial office space and at the same time providing refuge beneath these earthquake-resistant structures for automobiles and pedestrians caught in the open during severe earthquakes. With several of these structures available in the downtown areas, thousands of people could be saved from death and injury due to the collapse of older buildings in the vicinity.

Architects will be able to determine the optimum height of these new structures in order to balance the economic benefit of the additional office space with the safety benefit of structures most capable of remaining standing during severe earthquakes.

ARCHITECTURE IS WHAT YOU DO TO A BUILDING WHEN YOU LOOK AT IT.
—WALT WHITMAN

CHAPTER 25

Revitalizing America's Cities by Elevating Park Areas

Many areas of US cities could be revitalized through a program that would at the same time provide the cities with very substantial new sources of revenue. These improvements could be accomplished by auctioning off to the highest bidder certain downtown park areas that are currently poorly maintained and in many cases have become habitats of drug dealers, drug users, and homeless persons.

The winning developers of these valuable tracts of land would be allowed to construct commercial buildings no taller than the shortest building bordering the park. The top floor of the new construction would be required to replicate to some extent the original park design, including relocation of any monuments or fountains in place at the time of redevelopment.

In order to preserve even more natural beauty in the new structure, the city might require the builder to construct an exterior featuring a low-inclination ramp spiraling around the building from the ground floor to the park on the rooftop. At various intervals along the ramp could be located shrubbery and flower gardens, pieces of sculpture, restaurants, and picnic tables, giving the new park complex a capability for enhanced community development.

An additional feature could be a requirement that at least one of the floors of the new structure be reserved for residential use, thus contributing to the reduction of commuter traffic, bringing more life to the neighborhood and adding to the city's tax rolls.

> THE PURSUIT OF TRUTH AND BEAUTY IS A SPHERE OF ACTIVITY IN WHICH WE ARE PERMITTED TO REMAIN CHILDREN ALL OUR LIVES.
>
> —ALBERT EINSTEIN

CHAPTER 26

REDUCING THE NUMBER OF ACCIDENTS CAUSED BY MOTORISTS RUNNING RED LIGHTS

In the United States, approximately one thousand deaths, ninety thousand injuries, and hundreds of millions of dollars in damages are caused annually by motorists running red lights. The Federal Highway Administration has conducted a survey indicating that 96 percent of drivers fear being hit by a red light runner and that 56 percent of them admit to running red lights.

A significant reduction in these accidents could be achieved by a relatively simple measure that could be implemented easily and economically. Local traffic officials would measure the distance a vehicle traveling at the posted speed limit would cover from the time a traffic signal turned amber until it turned red. They would add to this distance the width of the intersection to be crossed and then mark off this distance from the intersection entrance in the direction of its approach. This segment of the street or highway would then be marked clearly with yellow stripes, creating a zone within which a vehicle approaching the intersection would be required to have entered in order to proceed through the intersection once the traffic signal has turned amber.

Any vehicle that has not entered the yellow-striped zone prior to the signal turning amber would be required to slow and come to a stop before entering the intersection once the traffic signal has turned green. This would discourage motorists from speeding up as soon as they see an amber light, hoping to cross the intersection before the signal turns red. But it would assure motorists who were traveling at or above the posted speed limit that if they were inside the marked zone when the signal turned amber, they could proceed through the intersection without increasing speed.

Officials with the authority to establish this procedure could almost overnight bring about a significant reduction in deaths, injuries, and damage caused by red light runners.

TO FLY, WE HAVE TO HAVE RESISTANCE.
—MAYA LIN

CHAPTER 27

A VAN FLEET RUNNING ON ELECTRIC POWER

This idea involves designing a commercial van that could operate to some extent like a hybrid car, using a smaller gasoline engine as well as braking forces to charge an array of batteries. It could also have a photovoltaic roof for additional battery-charging capabilities. But the principal feature would be to install seven or eight modules of five or six lead-acid batteries beneath the floor of the van.

Since the lithium batteries are still too expensive for installation in economically priced vehicles, and since the technology for lead-acid batteries is well advanced and well proven, these lead-acid battery modules could be installed in such a manner as to be quickly detached by a specially designed piece of support equipment (a cart) that could be slid under the van, where it would detach and remove the module. Another cart loaded with fully charged batteries would then be slid under the van, where it would attach the fresh module.

A complete change-out of the seven or eight modules could be accomplished in the same time it would take to refuel a conventional van. At the outset of demonstrating this concept, it would be wise to work out a cooperative arrangement perhaps with FedEx or UPS or the US Postal Service, where battery module exchange sites could be colocated with the companies' package-loading sites.

If these vans turn out to be as successful as I think they will, the manufacturer could later sell them for private use as well. For many commuters, the seven modules would be adequate for their commuter round trip and could be plugged in for recharge both at the worksite and at home. Operators of these vans could also be provided with the module-handling cart, so they could have a module charging at home during the day, which could be installed that evening at the end of the commuter run in case the driver needed to use the van for the evening before plugging it in for an overnight charge.

Service stations dedicated to changing out battery modules would also be developed, perhaps in conjunction with gasoline service stations, but I think stations devoted entirely to the replacement of battery modules and other service requirements specific to these vans would turn out to be more economical, especially since they would not need to participate in the cost of fuel-storage tanks and the high insurance rates associated with gasoline stations. Fleets of these vans would help the company that manufactures them meet the new stringent government requirements for improved fuel economy.

SCIENCE IS ORGANIZED KNOWLEDGE.
WISDOM IS ORGANIZED LIFE.
—IMMANUEL KANT

CHAPTER 28

HARNESSING THE ENERGY RELEASED BY GRAIN-DUST EXPLOSIONS

Every year in the United States there are a dozen or so grain-elevator explosions of great force, ignited by spark or flame. If this type of explosive mixture could be created within a cylinder or other strong vessel capable of containing the force of a controlled explosion, enabling a piston or other device (perhaps similar to the design of the Wankel engine) to transfer the energy into the generation of electricity or to the direct drive of a geared engine, perhaps this relatively plentiful fuel could help reduce the nation's dependence on the combustion of fossil fuels.

> DO NOT WAIT TO STRIKE TILL THE IRON IS
> HOT; BUT MAKE IT HOT BY STRIKING.
> —WILLIAM BUTLER YEATS

CHAPTER 29

RETIRING OVERAGE AIRCRAFT CARRIERS GRACEFULLY

This essay was composed in 2005. Although it dealt with the disposition of the aircraft carrier USS *John F. Kennedy* (CV 67), and was unsuccessful in providing a second, less-strenuous career for that illustrious ship, it is equally applicable for additional aircraft carriers scheduled for decommissioning.

The US Navy plans to put the USS *John F. Kennedy*, the newer of its two active nonnuclear aircraft carriers, in mothballs beginning in September. On April 19, Senators John Warner (R-Va.) and Bill Nelson (D-Fla.) introduced legislation to keep the *JFK* in service at least until mid-2006. A colloquy on the factors that led to the navy's decision was conducted by Warner, chairman of the Senate Armed Services Committee, and Admiral Vern Clark, chief of naval operations during a February 10 hearing on the Department of Defense's fiscal year 2006 budget.

Warner recalled that "when we were up against tough budget decisions," Sen. John Stennis (D-Miss.) would always recall to him, "How many times have I visited presidents of the United States and the presidents would always say, 'John, tell me about the carrier force, because when that phone rings at night, the first thing I think about is: Where is the nearest United States aircraft carrier?'"

Warner continued, "So you can imagine the surprise—if not shock—that was received here in the Congress with the arrival of the president's budget, where we're departing from that level of carriers—it's been … the integral building block, not only for the navy, but for our force structure and in our planning for forward-deployed operations—in the … proposed retirement in this budget by the president of the United States … of the *Kennedy*."

With the world situation so filled with uncertainty, and with the United States engaged in war in Iraq, Syria, and Afghanistan, and potential confrontation in the Baltic nations, Taiwan Strait, North Korea, Iran, and even Venezuela, it would appear that this is not the most efficacious moment to reduce the nation's carrier fleet. Here are some ideas for keeping the *Kennedy* out of mothballs for the next few years, and in a state from which she could be reintegrated into the fleet on relatively short notice but at considerably less expense than required to operate her with an air wing and a battle group.

First, maintain the *Kennedy* as a sea-based utility platform, with US Army Special Forces, Navy SEALs, and US Marines supported by helicopters and V-22 aircraft operating from her, providing services similar to the activities conducted during the initial phase of Operation Enduring Freedom by the USS *Kitty Hawk* in the Persian Gulf. In this role, without the need for operational catapults and arresting gear and some of the other capabilities required in a fully equipped operational strike carrier, the *Kennedy* would be less expensive to maintain and operate than she is currently.

Second, operate the *Kennedy* as a naval training center. Move some of the technical training courses for both officers and enlisted personnel to the ship, using these personnel as supplements to a relatively small permanent ship's company. Midshipmen from the naval academy and NROTC programs could participate, providing adequate numbers of junior officers. Postgraduate courses conducted by the Naval Postgraduate School at Monterey and the Naval War College in Newport could also be conducted on board, providing adequate numbers of more senior officers.

Third, offer the *Kennedy* to NATO as a truly multination asset. With each of the NATO nations bearing a share of the ship's operating expenses, as well as providing members of the crew, the cost to the United States would be reduced significantly, and NATO would possess a far more credible power-projection capability than it does today. An agreement with the other NATO nations to return the *Kennedy* to US naval service if required would be part of the arrangement.

Fourth, operate the *Kennedy* by the US Merchant Marine and the Department of Commerce as a marketing and goodwill platform, with the hangar bays and other spaces made available to US manufacturers and other industrial entities, to display their products at port visits worldwide.

By operating helicopters and V-22s, the Americans could move these vendors to fairs and expositions inland, especially in nations where US products are not currently available. Perhaps agreements could be made with nations visited by the ship to conduct business on a duty-free basis with US importers as well as exporters participating, thus promoting world trade and possibly reducing the current trade deficit.

These are possible means of keeping this magnificent ship from retirement right at this moment in history, when being able to quickly bring the fleet back up to its normal strength might be of great consequence.

Now, as other older aircraft carriers will be decommissioned in the next few years, they might become good candidates for one of the follow-on careers I suggested for the *JFK*.

BIG SHOTS ARE ONLY LITTLE SHOTS WHO KEEP SHOOTING.

—CHRISTOPHER MORLEY

CHAPTER 30

RELAY GOLF

This is a plan to give thousands of golfers and would-be golfers an opportunity to engage in the sport without the expense of traditional golf club membership and without the inconvenience associated with obtaining access to public golf courses.

Within most heavily populated metropolitan areas there are tracts of land that, although not of sufficient extent to support even nine typical golf course holes, would be adequate real estate to accommodate two or three typical par-four holes. The smallest of these venues would be a two-hole course with greens and tees at each end. Relay golf would be played on this truncated course in the following manner.

The game would be played by two four-man teams. Each team would position a player at four locations: (1) the tee to the first hole; (2) on the fairway approximately three hundred yards from the tee; (3) near the green in position to play the approach shot; and (4) on the number-one green itself. After the players on the number-one green have holed out, they would tee off back up the fairway. In the meantime the players who had made the approach shot would move back up the fairway becoming the group assigned to make the second shot to hole number two (in the vicinity of the tee to hole number one). The group that had played the second shot on the way to hole number one would now play the approach shot to hole number two. The twosome that had made the original drive from the number-one tee would now do the putting on the number-two green. While they were putting out, the twosome that had made the approach shot would take position on the number-one tee, to be replaced on the fairway by the putting twosome. At the same time or earlier, the putting twosome on the number-one green would trade places with the twosome that had made the second shot, who would now become the putters for the third hole and the drivers for the fourth hole.

This alternating of positions would continue through play of nine or eighteen holes. On tracts of land that could support three holes, a similar playing procedure would be employed by playing three holes in succession and then reversing the field as in the two-hole procedure.

Relay golf could result in the development of close-knit four-person teams competing frequently on these more accessible two- and three-hole courses that could be easily developed on tracts of land within large metropolitan areas. Some of these courses would probably evolve into golf clubs, complete with the amenities available at traditional golf clubs. Relay golf would have special appeal for inner-city youth, who would not only have this unique opportunity to be introduced more accessibly to golf but would enjoy the heightened competitiveness of this faster-moving version of the sport.

There will almost surely be opposition to the implementation of relay golf by golf traditionalists. This opposition was anticipated by John Locke: "New opinions are always suspected, and usually opposed, without any other reason but because they are not already common."

A SMILE IS THE CHOSEN VEHICLE FOR ALL AMBIGUITIES.

—HERMAN MELVILLE

CHAPTER 31

SALVAGING FLORIDA'S TIRE REEFS

A plan to create artificial reefs composed of used automobile tires has not worked out well off the eastern coast of Florida, where over a period of several years approximately two million tires have been dumped. Some of the tires were moved by ocean currents and storms in such a way as to damage natural coral reefs, already under stress from pollution and other conditions. Later, an expensive campaign was conducted to remove the tires from the ocean floor.

An alternative to this program has the potential for accomplishing what the original plan was designed to do: create solid structures on the ocean floor that provide refuge for certain species of fish and other ocean inhabitants. This plan will also provide interesting work for the divers who have engaged in removing the tires. Instead of removing the tires, the divers should be shown how to create relatively permanent tire reefs that will resist the pressures of ocean currents and storms. This will be done by creating tubular arrays of tires lashed together with nylon line that is very resistant to decomposition in salt water and filling these arrays with silt and/or sand scraped and dredged from the adjacent ocean floor.

The tires should be formed into a variety of designs so that the efficacy of the different patterns can be observed and then replicated throughout the expanse of ocean where the tires are located. One likely form for these reefs would be a pattern wherein three rows of tires would be laid out adjacent to each other, interlaced with nylon line to hold them together. On top of the center row of tires would be attached another layer of tires, sometimes just one tire high, but occasionally an additional tire attached on top of this row, creating a reef of irregular height, but with all the tires filled with silt or sand from the ocean floor.

The cavities in the ocean floor created by the divers equipped with buckets or other tools will also provide habitat for certain ocean creatures, as well as nesting areas for some of the fish that spawn in the area.

This concept should be tried out in various forms. Perhaps a circular pattern twenty to thirty tires in diameter might turn out to be an attractive reef for the ocean dwellers. It could be arranged in a sort of stair-step fashion that would extend possibly eight or ten tire layers high. This design would be more resistant to ocean currents than would horizontal arrays. However, the linear arrays, constructed as barriers to the movement tires are currently experiencing, should cause a buildup of migrating tires piling up against this much more stable array of tire cylinders filled with silt and sand, resulting in the kind of tire reef envisioned years ago.

Divers could continue to add more layers of sand- or silt-filled tires in order to maintain a barrier high enough to trap all migrating tires. The barrier patterns should be located strategically in such a way as to protect the natural reefs from migrating tires. Admittedly, the positioning of tires, the lacing of them together, and the scooping up of silt and sand from the ocean floor to fill them up will be tedious work, but many volunteer divers will find this to be a far more creative and productive achievement than simply assisting in the removal of the two million tires. They could be assisted in filling the tire cylinders by boats on the surface dragging scraper buckets across the ocean floor, scooping up silt and sand and then releasing it onto the tire cylinder array. Once these arrays of cylinders of tires are filled with sand and silt, they will become stable enough to resist ocean currents and storm-churned seas, and as more and more of the two million migrating tires pile up behind them, they will become increasingly larger barrier reefs, protective habitat for multitudes of sea creatures.

PEOPLE, EVEN MORE THAN THINGS, HAVE TO BE RESTORED, RENEWED, REVIVED, RECLAIMED AND REDEEMED; NEVER THROW OUT ANYONE.
—AUDREY HEPBURN

CHAPTER 32

SAVING THE SALTON SEA

This plan has potential for restoring the Salton Sea to its earlier state, when it provided one of California's best recreational areas. The sea is rapidly diminishing in area and is becoming too salty to sustain its fish population.

My idea is to construct a siphon pipeline from the Pacific Ocean or from the Gulf of California in such a way as to take advantage of the Salton Sea's below-sea-level elevation. By siphoning in the ocean water, the shrinking volume of the sea would be reversed, and its salinity and contamination from other minerals would be diluted to the point that would support the level of fish survivability that existed earlier. It would also make the Salton Sea more desirable for swimming and other watersports.

Although I lack the engineering background to calculate whether hydroelectric generators could be installed in the lower sections of the pipeline, if that turns out to be feasible, I can see potential hydroelectric power output from this process.

If a small experimental pipeline were constructed and found feasible, multiple larger pipelines could be developed to maximize the benefit. There may be scientific reasons why this idea isn't feasible. That would explain why it hasn't been proposed before. But perhaps with the advances that have been made recently in pipeline construction and in electrical generators, the time may be ripe for an experimental installation. Maybe the Dead Sea would be another candidate for this idea.

> WHEN I WAS A BOY THE DEAD SEA WAS ONLY SICK.
>
> —GEORGE BURNS

CHAPTER 33

A New Source of Electricity for New Orleans

Over the last century or so, the lower Mississippi River, by virtue of siltation and ever higher levees, has risen well above sea level as it passes through New Orleans. This is a plan that can produce clean, low-cost electrical power for New Orleans and the lower Mississippi area and at the same time restore the normal silting process that used to enrich the Mississippi Delta. It will also reduce the impact of the toxic outflow of the Mississippi River into the Gulf of Mexico.

The plan is to install a series of hydroelectric generators in the levees of the right bank of the river, where there is enough of a drop from the normal height of the river down to outflow canals near sea level to generate an economically feasible amount of electricity. Each generator outflow would empty into a canal that would lead to the most appropriate creek or swamp in the area, where these high-nutrient and high-silt-bearing waters would wind their way to the Gulf of Mexico, dropping their silt and enriching the delta as they did before man straightened the river's course. The array of generator sluices along the levee would also have beneficial effects on flood control, by allowing the Army Corps of Engineers, or whatever other authority is given the responsibility, to bring more generators online when river levels rise above optimal levels and to close them off during periods of low water.

Over the years, the silt from these waters will once again build up the delta, providing the buffering that helped New Orleans survive hurricanes over earlier centuries. This same plan could be applied to the Yangtze and Yellow rivers in China, where they have experienced the same phenomenon as New Orleans.

> IMAGINATION IS MORE IMPORTANT THAN KNOWLEDGE.
>
> —ALBERT EINSTEIN

CHAPTER 34

Reducing the Cost of "The War on Drugs" While Reducing Prison Populations and Enhancing the Environment

For a fraction of the amount the federal and state governments spend on the war on drugs, they could develop a program that would have a significant effect on reducing the consumption of illegal drugs in the United States and at the same time bring about a reduction in prison populations while reducing flooding and improving water quality nationwide as discussed in chapter 9.

Instead of automatically sending persons convicted of drug possession to prison, they would be given the opportunity to volunteer for assignment to hydrologic redevelopment teams. The teams would deploy along designated waterways as described in chapter 9, where they would engage in developing the shallow impoundments along the banks of rivers, streams, creeks, and ravines that would collect water that flows over the streams' banks during periods of heavy rainfall and runoff.

These construction teams, composed of volunteer prisoners who have not committed violent crimes, would be supervised by government officials who are trained not only in the conservation field but also as prison guards. There would be one of these officials for every ten volunteers, and these officials would keep careful records of the performance of each volunteer. The volunteers would be informed that for every day of satisfactory performance evaluated by the supervising official, their prison sentence would be reduced by two days, and for outstanding performance the reduction would be three days.

Volunteers who are apprehended with drugs or commit other illegal actions will have their sentences increased in proportion to the offense. If their behavior is considered disruptive to the team's overall performance, they will be sent to prison to complete the remainder of their sentence.

The volunteers will have collateral duties such as cooking, camp maintenance, latrine construction, and so forth, following the procedures established by the Civilian Conservation Corps during the 1930s.

Since many of the volunteers will be young men and women who have never held a steady job before, this experience will prepare them for reentry into society with work habits that will assist them in obtaining and keeping gainful employment. Judges who are reluctant to send first- or even second-time drug offenders to prescribed prison terms of considerable length and therefore let them off with probation would be more inclined to send them off to the conservation program, to the benefit of both the felon and society.

NEVER DOUBT THAT A SMALL GROUP OF THOUGHTFUL CITIZENS CAN CHANGE THE WORLD. INDEED, IT IS THE ONLY THING THAT EVER HAS.

—MARGARET MEAD

CHAPTER 35

SAVING THE FEDERAL GOVERNMENT MILLIONS OF DOLLARS BY MINTING PLASTIC PENNIES

It costs the federal government more than the value of a copper penny to manufacture one. This unnecessary drain on the nation's finances could be avoided by manufacturing pennies from plastic. Several financial benefits in addition to the one related to the difference in cost of penny manufacture will accrue from this change. Once the populace knows that there will be no more copper pennies produced, a large number of pennies will be withdrawn from circulation by coin collectors. Millions of the new plastic pennies will also be withdrawn from circulation each year by collectors; this volume could be amplified if the head of a different dignitary were to appear on the coin each year.

> GOOD ADVICE IS SOMETHING A MAN GIVES
> WHEN HE IS TOO OLD TO SET A BAD EXAMPLE.
> —FRANCOIS DE LA ROCHEFOUCAULD

CHAPTER 36

ADVICE FOR WAITRESSES, WAITERS, MANAGERS, AND OWNERS OF RESTAURANTS

I have dined at hundreds of restaurants all over the United States, Europe, and Asia and have noticed one adverse characteristic displayed in approximately half the US establishments I've visited and to a lesser extent in those abroad, that if eliminated, would result in larger tips and more return visits to the restaurant.

This unsatisfactory trait is simply the failure of waitresses and waiters to look around the dining area before returning to the kitchen after serving one table. A quick glance around the area would allow other diners who may be ready to receive their check or otherwise require attention to be attended to without excessive delay.

As I develop my analysis of these incidents, I will refer to the more professional and attentive server, who is found in approximately half the restaurants in the United States as Server 1. This quality of server would always glance around the dining area after taking the order or otherwise serving a particular table.

If a table where diners require attention is the responsibility of Server 1, he would stop at that table before proceeding to the kitchen. If the table is the responsibility of another server, Server 1 would approach the table to find out what is desired or at least make eye contact with the diners at that table, and nodding to them, indicate that he would inform the responsible server of their need.

This problem is less likely to manifest itself in the more expensive restaurants, especially in France, Spain, Italy, Singapore, Hong Kong, and Japan. In these locales the profession of waiter or waitress is more highly regarded than it is in the United States, where service-industry jobs are far more frequently filled by inattentive part-time employees, who may have other things on their minds, to the exclusion of ensuring the efficiency and success of the establishment.

Most restaurant managers probably instruct their servers to operate in the manner of Server 1, but it is obvious that not all of them follow through to ensure that this level of performance is maintained.

A restaurant where the attributes of Server 1 are not in evidence could improve its customer satisfaction and profitability appreciably by simply ensuring that this method of surveillance and response is second nature to its serving staff.

THE MAIN THING IS TO CARE. CARE VERY HARD, EVEN IF IT IS ONLY A GAME YOU ARE PLAYING.

—BILLIE JEAN KING

CHAPTER 37

THE NEXT BOMBER FOR THE UNITED STATES AIR FORCE

The US Air Force is planning to develop a new bomber scheduled to enter service in 2025. Eighty to a hundred strike aircraft are planned at a cost of $550 million each. This will be a stealthy, penetrating bomber, capable of persisting over hostile territory.

A bomber much better suited to the threats that will face the United States in the future would be a modification of one of the newest large commercial aircraft such as Boeing's 787.

Instead of wasting billions of developmental dollars on a new combination of stealth, supersonic design, and advanced engines, some of these dollars could be utilized more effectively by developing hypersonic air-to-surface missiles that could be delivered in far greater numbers from these new large-body bombers than could be accomplished by penetrating bombers.

The large bombers should also be multimission aircraft. One of their roles might be to operate within range of aircraft carriers, where the bomber could serve as an airborne command center escorted by fighters from the carrier. The bomber could also be equipped with long-range air-to-air missiles and should be capable of refueling both manned and unmanned aircraft.

Potential enemies are devoting tremendous efforts to the development of air-defense networks capable of detecting and attacking stealthy bombers. By the time a new penetrating bomber could be deployed, there is no assurance that it could deal effectively with these air-defense networks. However, the large airliner-type bomber, escorted by carrier-based fighters and equipped with large numbers of long-range hypersonic missiles, or in the near term, slower but stealthy long-range missiles would be far more capable of saturating enemy air defenses and carrying out successful airstrikes.

> TO FIND WHAT YOU SEEK IN THE ROAD OF LIFE, THE BEST PROVERB OF ALL IS THAT WHICH SAYS: "LEAVE NO STONE UNTURNED."
> —EDWARD BULWER-LYTTON

CHAPTER 38

ENABLING WHEELCHAIR OCCUPANTS TO NEGOTIATE CURBS AND STEPS

Wheelchairs could be equipped with a metal ramp that might be stowed in a slot on the back of the chair, where the occupant could reach back and withdraw it from the stowage slot when required. The ramp would have a fold-out brace that would provide adequate reinforcement once in place. The occupant would position the ramp so that its forward edge would rest on the curb or step to be climbed. This edge would lie flat on top of the curb and would then curve down at an appropriate angle, making the climb a relatively easy effort for the average wheelchair occupant. The upper surface of the ramp would have a rough surface that would prevent the wheels from slipping. The occupant would also be equipped with a rod with a hook on its end so that he could position and retrieve the ramp by inserting this hook into a recessed fitting. A wheelchair thus equipped would allow its occupant to proceed through hundreds of streets and sidewalks that have not yet been modified for wheelchair access.

IF YOU COME TO A FORK IN THE ROAD, TAKE IT.
—YOGI BERRA

CHAPTER 39

NEW PRISONS ORGANIZED FOR REHABILITATION RATHER THAN PUNISHMENT

Two million people are being supported in America's prisons, at great expense to the nation's taxpayers. Although a few prisons have developed programs successful in developing some of the prisoners' skills and attitudes that may enable them to integrate themselves successfully back into society, the vast majority of the prisons provide little more than custody.

Many prisoners who have been convicted of nothing more than drug possession or other nonviolent offenses emerge from prison years later as more capable and dangerous criminals, having become members of gangs led in prison by hardened repeat offenders, who have nothing better to do in prison than lifting weights, knifing an occasional inmate, and instructing gang members on how to operate in the gang's affiliate on the outside once released.

Prisoners should be obligated to work while they are in prison and should be given opportunities to improve their quality of life and to shorten their sentences by progressively improving performance.

Private industry should be invited to establish factories adjacent to the prisons, where products that are no longer manufactured elsewhere in the United States would be produced by the prisoners. There are multiple advantages to this program.

The prisoners would develop good work habits and learn skills that would assist them in becoming reintegrated in society upon completion of their sentences.

The products manufactured in these prison factories could be priced below similar products manufactured abroad, thus reducing the trade deficit.

By reestablishing manufacturing capability for several products that are no longer made in the United States, the nation's economy will have some resilience should foreign producers decide to restrict exports to the United States, for example in time of war.

With viable industries springing up around US prisons, there will be an economic boost to these areas from the establishment of component suppliers, transportation facilities, and other related activities.

As the prisoners become more like traditional workers and managers than like traditional prisoners, the numbers of guards and other supervisory prison personnel can be reduced.

If the prisoners are allowed to earn credits toward early release and attain early release for good performance, the overall prison population will be reduced, resulting in reduced state expense.

Every prisoner, including those kept in solitary confinement because of the potential danger to other prisoners, should be obligated to put in eight hours of work daily. This work could be as simple as sweeping floors or walking on a treadmill to generate electricity. Prisoners unwilling to participate in the work program should be provided less comfortable surroundings and less appetizing food than they could attain through cooperation with authorities.

WORK IS EITHER FUN OR DRUDGERY. IT DEPENDS ON YOUR ATTITUDE.
—COLLEEN C. BARRETT

CHAPTER 40

A Pleasant Method of Losing Weight

Having run across a magazine article that explained how sipping a cold drink while eating could result in less weight gain, I combined this procedure with a compatible dining style and found that over a six-month period, I managed to lose ten pounds without any dietary change.

The procedure I developed was to take smaller-than-usual bites of food and to chew and swallow each bite and then take a sip of ice water or a cold drink before taking the next bite. If I had one or more dining partners, I would also ask a question or make a comment after every second or third bite.

Because this procedure lengthened my dining time, I found my appetite satisfied after consuming slightly less quantity than had been the case prior to adopting the new style of eating. To verify the reason for my weight loss, I reverted to my previous eating style for three months and regained five pounds. Then I resumed the slower eating procedures and once more found them to be successful in reducing weight.

During evening meals I customarily enjoy a glass of wine or beer. Since I prefer red wine, I sometimes have sangria. I take alternate sips of sangria, wine, or beer with sips of ice water. Since I intersperse the bites and sips with questions or comments to fellow diners, I find them expounding on these stimuli enough to slow their own consumption of food and drink, thus leading to a more pleasant and satisfying dining experience than usual.

THE BEST THINGS IN LIFE AREN'T THINGS.
—ART BUCHWALD

CHAPTER 41

A CONVENIENT PROGRAM FOR
BUYING AND SELLING USED CARS

This is a program that could bring a new form of business to companies such as Wal-Mart, Sears, and other stores that have auto-service departments. The idea is to offer customers the opportunity to buy and sell used cars in a process coordinated by the participating company. The process would begin with the customer turning over his car to the company for a thorough checkup, to ensure it is roadworthy. Following the checkup, the service manager would inform the prospective seller of any repairs that would have to be completed before the car receives company certification. If the car needs no repair or after the recommended repairs have been made, the car will be parked in a specially designated section of the company's parking area or the adjacent mall parking area. In the car or truck window will be a poster with all the vehicle's vital statistics, including the owner's asking price, special equipment, mileage, and so forth. If the seller is willing to accept less than the asking price, the poster should note that the best offer may acquire the car.

Prospective sellers would have the option of leaving their car on display with the company for as much time as they want, checking it in and out with the company at their own convenience. This would allow a seller to use the car during the day, bring it to the lot after work, pick it up at evening closing time, drive it the next day, repeat the evening display process when convenient, and perhaps leave it on display the entire weekend. In order to move the inventory and not spend too much administrative time on any individual car, the host company might require the owner to reduce the asking price by a given amount each day or each week. This procedure would have the benefit of luring potential buyers back to the sales lot, hoping to acquire the car they are interested in after it comes down to the price they are willing to pay.

In addition to the money the company would earn from the checkup repair/certification process as well as a commission on the vehicle sale, it would benefit from having hundreds of potential auto sellers and buyers and their family members constantly wandering around the company's other departments, shopping for other merchandise. This whole process should turn out to be a very favorable public-relations achievement for the participating company, providing a valuable service to both auto buyers and sellers.

> WHEN PEOPLE KEEP TELLING YOU THAT YOU CAN'T DO A THING, YOU KIND OF LIKE TO TRY IT.
>
> —MARGARET CHASE SMITH

CHAPTER 42

EVACUATING PORT AND RIVER CITIES SUCH AS NEW YORK CITY AND WASHINGTON, DC, UNDER ATTACK BY WEAPONS OF MASS DESTRUCTION

Osama bin Laden and Ayman al-Zawahiri cosigned a fatwa in the name of the World Islamic Front for jihad against Jews and crusaders, which declared the killing of the Americans and their allies an "individual duty for every Muslim." At the public announcement of the fatwa, bin Laden noted that Americans are "very easy targets." He has since proved to be correct in his assertion, and from time to time his successors have reiterated his threats to kill more Americans. Those who have studied the activities of Al-Qaeda and the Islamic State are particularly worried about possible attacks by terrorists on cities such as New York and Washington, DC, featuring nuclear, biological, and chemical weapons of mass destruction.

Hurricanes Katrina and Rita have revealed the inadequacies of evacuation plans for the Gulf Coast. It is unlikely that whatever current plans that may exist for evacuating New York City, Washington, or any other city accessible by water are any better. But these cities have a great untapped evacuation resource that could, with adequate planning, allow a relatively safe and orderly exit of thousands of residents of the cities, who without such a plan would very likely be stranded in the cities by traffic jams on all land routes. These resources are the commercially and privately operated boats operating or moored within a mile or two of these cities. Plans to optimize the use of rivers and coastal waterways as evacuation routes should include the following details.

Agreements will be made with the owners of currently available watercraft to report to designated embarkation points when directed. These agreements can be of two types: Some boat owners may be willing to take on passengers for a one-way cruise to a debarkation point downstream or upstream but might not be willing to return for subsequent trips. Other owners, especially those who operate commercial boats, may be willing to sign agreements to shuttle between designated embarkation points and debarkation points considered to be outside the danger zone.

Arrangements should be made with one or more companies to operate ferry boats between embarkation and debarkation points. Some of these ferry boats would be configured to carry automobiles during their normal daily operations but would be available to take on larger numbers of pedestrians during emergency evacuations.

Military boats, operated by reservists, should be acquired and moored at military facilities such as the Washington Navy Yard, Fort Belvoir, Indian Head, and Quantico, near Washington, DC, and the former Brooklyn Naval Shipyard and similar facilities near New York. Military reserve units in the area, especially those of the US Coast Guard, would have the responsibility of coordinating the water evacuation of personnel during emergencies.

Rehearsals of emergency evacuations should be conducted at least semiannually, employing assets discussed in each of the above-listed elements. Well-qualified harbormasters located at the embarkation points and at each of the debarkation points should be equipped with radios and cell phones and with communication plans capable of ensuring contact with all participants. The Department of Homeland Security should organize monthly drills involving the harbormasters and smaller groups of the evacuation assets.

This plan could be implemented in part in a matter of weeks and expanded as more formal plans are developed. America's port and river cities need not wait for an emergency to occur before coming to grips with the evacuation problem.

> HE WHO REFUSES TO EMBRACE A UNIQUE OPPORTUNITY LOSES THE PRIZE AS SURELY AS IF HE HAD TRIED AND FAILED.
>
> —WILLIAM JAMES

CHAPTER 43

RESOLVING CONFLICTS: PRIORITIZED LISTS

This approach could be applied to conflicts between nations, between labor and management, between opposing political parties, and between individuals and organizations that need to settle disputes. The key to this program is the preparation of prioritized lists. Here is how the prioritized lists would be used to resolve conflicts.

1. An objective moderating team would suggest to the two conflicted parties that with their cooperation it would be possible to make gradual progress in resolving the conflict, and the two conflicting parties would agree to participate with no preset conditions.

2. An objective moderator would meet with the responsible representative of conflicted party A and would ask that the representative list, in descending order of importance, every action that conflicted party B would have to carry out in order to terminate the conflict.

3. While the evolution described in 2 is under way, a second objective moderator would carry out the same procedure with conflicted party B.

4. After the two conflicted parties have completed their lists, the objective moderators would deliver these lists to the opposing parties

and ask them to match any actions from the opponent's list that they would be willing to carry out in exchange for a matching action on their own list.

5. After completion of the procedure outlined in 4, the two conflicted parties would meet and agree to implement any of the actions that have resulted from the matching process.

6. The two conflicted parties would then implement the actions agreed upon and would also agree to revise the lists of actions for which no match had been achieved and to provide the revised lists to the opposing party.

7. After the actions outlined in 6 are completed, the conflicted parties would meet again and agree to implement any of the actions that have resulted from the matching process.

8. The implementation of matching actions and the constant revision of the prioritized lists following each implementation period would continue as long as the conflicted parties agree to participate. At some point, it would become clear whether the basic conflict could be resolved at all, but over the period of mutually agreed-upon action matching, it is possible that tensions between the conflicted parties would be reduced enough to enable a final successful resolution of the conflict.

IT'S NEVER TOO LATE TO GIVE UP YOUR PREJUDICES.

—HENRY DAVID THOREAU

CHAPTER 44

FRAUD-RESISTANT INSURANCE

The Coalition against Insurance Fraud estimates that in recent years, a total of about $80 billion was lost annually in the United States to insurance fraud. According to estimates by the Insurance Information Institute, insurance fraud accounts for 10 percent, or about $30 billion, of losses in the property and casualty insurance industries in the United States.

The Insurance Research Council estimated that in several years, 21 to 36 percent of auto-insurance claims contained elements of suspected fraud. As millions of owners of businesses, homes, motor vehicles, and boats find themselves owing more to their lenders than their possessions are worth, there is an even greater temptation to resort to insurance fraud as a means of escape.

In order to absorb these losses, insurance companies can be expected to increase their rates substantially, leading to even greater financial hardship for honest home, business, and motor-vehicle owners. I propose a new form of fraud-resistant insurance that will reduce the insurers' risk considerably, while allowing them to pass these savings on to their insured clients. The new policies will contain a clause by which the insured agrees to a polygraph interview before the payment of any claim.

At the time the insured files a claim of loss, and prior to payment by the insurer, the claimant will voluntarily submit to a polygraph interview and will respond to every question concerning the loss. The results of the polygraph interview are not admissible as evidence in a court of law, even if they indicate that the insurance claim is fraudulent, but if indeed the claim is fraudulent, the interview may very likely reveal clues that investigators can use in discovering the fraud.

It is not anticipated that the primary source of savings to the insurers will come from polygraph-detected fraud but from the fact that the vast majority of the purchasers of fraud-resistant policies will either have no intent to defraud the insurers at the time they purchase the policy or, if they are later tempted to commit fraud, they will be deterred because of the possibility that the polygraph interview would expose their fraud.

Not every potential purchaser of property and casualty insurance will take advantage of the fraud-resistant policies, but those who purchase them and those who issue them will derive considerable benefit. It is quite likely that the overall losses to the US economy due to insurance fraud will decline, accompanied by a reduction in the costs of theft and arson investigations to local governments.

> INSURANCE—AN INGENIOUS MODERN GAME OF CHANCE IN WHICH THE PLAYER IS PERMITTED TO ENJOY THE COMFORTABLE CONVICTION THAT HE IS BEATING THE MAN WHO KEEPS THE TABLE.
>
> —AMBROSE BIERCE

CHAPTER 45

AVOIDING REAR-END COLLISIONS IN FOG

Every year thousands of rear-end collisions occur during periods of fog, many of them serious chain-reaction pileups involving as many as seventy vehicles. The number and severity of these accidents could be reduced appreciably if vehicles frequently driven on fog-prone highways were equipped with a warning device. This device would be a translucent plastic alarm ball at the end of a sixty-foot cable. The ball would contain a light source powered either through the suspension cable or charged by the motion of the ball bouncing along the highway surface. The dispenser component of the device would be capable of retracting the cable and alarm ball once the vehicle has exited the fog area.

Since it is unlikely that every vehicle entering an area of dense fog would be equipped with one of these devices or with other devices such as radar sensors, there will continue to be many rear-end collisions, but at least the vehicles so equipped will be less likely to be hit, and even if hit, the impact speed would be reduced due to the increased braking distance afforded the approaching vehicle alerted by the bouncing, flashing alarm ball.

HINDSIGHT IS ALWAYS 20/20.
—BILLY WILDER

CHAPTER 46

REPLACING PLASTIC SHOPPING BAGS WITH BAGS OF FABRIC

Millions of dollars currently being spent by grocery stores for plastic shopping bags could be saved by replacing these bags with reusable fabric bags. Many nationwide grocery chains such as Whole Foods and Harris Teeter, as well as the military commissaries, are already selling these bags, but usage to date is relatively limited.

If the grocery stores would deduct one or two cents from the grocery bill for each cloth bag bearing the store's logo, this would incentivize shoppers to buy and use the cloth bags and would provide favorable advertising for the grocery stores.

An additional incentive could be a one- or two-cent charge for each paper or plastic bag provided at checkout. As the transition from plastic and paper bags to reusable fabric bags develops, three very significant benefits to the nation's economy and to its environment will occur.

1. Millions of barrels of oil currently consumed in the production of plastic bags will become available for refining into gasoline, diesel, or home-heating fuel, relieving cost pressure on these products.
2. Millions of dollars currently being spent on collection and disposal of plastic and paper bags will be saved, resulting in a reduction in household and community expenses.

3. The number of plastic bags that are currently finding their way into waterways, oceans, and other areas where they cause the deaths of millions of fish, turtles, birds, and other wildlife will be reduced significantly—an overall benefit to the environment.

Even though the advantages achieved through implementation of this concept will be readily apparent to most grocery store owners and managers and to many of their customers, this would be an excellent opportunity for chambers of commerce and consumer organizations to conduct campaigns promoting it.

> IF YOU'RE NOT A RISK TAKER, YOU SHOULD
> GET THE HELL OUT OF BUSINESS.
> —RAY KROC

CHAPTER 47

ELIMINATING PIRATES FROM THE GULF OF ADEN AND INDIAN OCEAN

The solution to the problem of piracy could be relatively inexpensive, yet very effective. It could also provide excellent combat training for US Navy, Marine Corps, and Special Forces personnel. The idea is to revive the Q-ship concept employed by Great Britain's Royal Navy (and to a lesser extent by Germany and the United States) in World War I and II, whereby merchant ships were equipped with concealed weaponry and operated so as to lure enemy submarines into making surface attacks. This gave the Q-ships the chance to open fire and sink them. The basic ethos of every Q-ship was to be a wolf in sheep's clothing. During World War I, British Royal Navy Q-ships fought one hundred fifty engagements, destroying fourteen U-boats and damaging sixty, at a cost of twenty-seven Q-ships lost out of two hundred. Today's Q-ships should acquire a more successful combat record, in that the Somali pirates have far less capability than did German U-boats.

Although the World War II Q-ships were less successful than those of World War I, one of them might serve as the model for Somali operations. Here is her description from the US Naval Historical Society's adaptation of a reference from *Eastern Sea Frontier War Diary*, October 1943, ch. 2, "Queen

Ships" pp 9–34. Modern Military Branch, National Archives and Records
Administration, 8601 Adelphi Road, College Park, MD 20740:

> The most formidable of the Q-ships was the tanker SS *Gulf
> Dawn*, selected by Commander Eastern Sea Frontier after
> Cominch had approved his proposal for using a disguised
> tanker. Conversion was begun in March 1942 at the
> Bethlehem 56th Street Brooklyn Yard and was continued at
> the Navy Yard Boston, where the work was finally completed
> on July 22, 1942. Equipment included five 4-inch .50 caliber
> single purpose guns, two .50 caliber machine guns, five
> "Tommy" guns, five sawed-off shotguns, one Model JK-9
> listening equipment. She was commissioned USS *Big Horn*
> (AO-45).

A twenty-first-century version of USS *Big Horn* could make piracy in the
Arabian Sea a very risky occupation for Somali pirates.

PICK BATTLES BIG ENOUGH TO MATTER, SMALL ENOUGH TO WIN.
—JONATHAN KOZOL

CHAPTER 48

REVIVING DORMANT INDUSTRIES

The federal government could energize the United States economy very quickly by a simple change in the way unemployment compensation is provided. US- or foreign-owned companies would be given the following incentives to manufacture any item that is not currently manufactured in the United States, thereby not incurring the wrath of organized labor or competitive industries in the United States.

Candidate companies could establish manufacturing plants anywhere in the United States where they determine that there are enough currently unemployed workers to provide an adequate workforce. Once these companies are prepared to hire the necessary workforce, the federal government would pay unemployment compensation only to personnel who accept employment at the new companies. The new companies would be required to pay the workers the same compensation being paid by the lowest-cost producer of the manufactured item anywhere in the world. The workers would receive this compensation in addition to the unemployment compensation provided by the government, but since the labor costs to the new companies would be no more than those of the low-cost foreign producer, these companies should quickly gain market share, having shipping and ancillary expenses far lower than their foreign competitors.

Workers accepting employment at the new companies would be offered flexible working hours so they would have a few hours each week to conduct employment interviews with potential employers in their former skill areas, but they would be required to work a forty-hour week with the new company in order to be paid their unemployment compensation.

As more and more of these companies begin taking back market share of their respective manufactured items, they will become increasingly profitable. In order for them to stay profitable, and in recognition of their contribution to the improving economy, these new companies should be guaranteed exemption from corporate income tax for a period of ten years and not be required to provide health care or retirement benefits.

But since there will always be thousands of otherwise-unemployed workers, each of these companies should find an adequate workforce as long as the federal government requires unemployed workers to work in these plants in order to receive unemployment compensation.

> A LIFE SPENT MAKING MISTAKES IS NOT ONLY
> MORE HONORABLE BUT MORE USEFUL THAN
> A LIFE SPENT DOING NOTHING.
> —GEORGE BERNARD SHAW

CHAPTER 49

REVIVING SMALL HYDROELECTRIC POWER PROGRAMS

Reestablishing small hydroelectric plants (as well as developing new ones) has the potential for providing substantial environmentally friendly sources of electricity. I grew up in Loup City, Nebraska (population at that time 1,675), and remember that the city's power was provided during daylight hours until about four thirty in the afternoon by a small hydroelectric power plant at Lake Ericson, about seventy miles distant. The power was generated through a dam on the Cedar River that formed Lake Ericson. At four thirty, I suppose when the water level at the lake had become too low to power the turbine, a diesel generator in Loup City came online until Lake Ericson had filled again to a level capable of powering the turbine. This power plant provided electricity for several communities until the 1970s.

Not far from Loup City, a hydroelectric power plant on the Middle Loup River at Boelus also produced electricity. Since much of the Loup River's water is now diverted to irrigation canals in the summer, a reconstructed Boelus operation would probably be feasible only for operations throughout the months when irrigation is not taking place. However, I have a plan for creating lakes similar to Lake Ericson within the banks of wide sandbar-configured rivers such as the Loup and Platte rivers in Nebraska.

This plan would be accomplished by constructing dikes or levees along the banks of these rivers using dredge spoil from the riverbeds. The lakes would extend for whatever length is necessary to provide adequate head pressure to produce electricity. A series of these lakes all across Nebraska on the Loup and Platte rivers would provide a tremendous amount of electricity, contributing immensely to the nation's needs for renewable sources of energy.

The lakes would also provide great recreational benefits. Since many of them could be constructed along the Platte River adjacent to Interstate 80, Nebraska could become a marvelous environment for fishing, boating, and camping for tourists transiting what is considered by many today as a boring and dismal segment of their journey.

Similar hydroelectric facilities could be developed along narrow rivers with high banks, such as the Big Blue River in Nebraska and Kansas. The plan for these rivers would be to construct dams on them, forcing the water into a new channel created by a levee constructed on one of the riverbanks.

The new channel would run parallel to the river for a distance adequate to provide for a sufficient drop to the original riverbed to generate electricity. The lakes and new channels formed by this process would also add recreational assets to the environment.

Whereas rivers such as the Big Blue are difficult to access because of their steep banks, by diverting the flow to a new channel on higher ground parallel to the old riverbed, the new channel would become more accessible to fishermen and boaters. The power plants could be constructed in a similar manner to the Loup Power Canal facilities currently in service at the Monroe Powerhouse and the Columbus Powerhouse in Nebraska.

In addition to providing a great new source of energy and recreation for Nebraska, these plans could save millions of dollars currently being paid by Nebraskans for electricity delivered from out of state or generated within the state from imported coal or natural gas.

Although this chapter was aimed at reviving hydroelectric power in Nebraska, this thesis is applicable to every state in the Union and every nation in the world with rivers similar to the ones described here.

MAN SHAPES HIMSELF THROUGH DECISIONS
THAT SHAPE HIS ENVIRONMENT.
—RENE DUBOS

CHAPTER 50

IMPROVING FUEL MILEAGE
IN EIGHTEEN-WHEELERS

I have an idea that by mounting a winglike airfoil on the top of eighteen-wheeler trailers, enough lift would be generated to reduce the apparent weight of the trailer and thereby increase the truckers' mileage per gallon. In addition to the cumulative savings in the cost of diesel fuel, there would be a reduction in downtime for refueling and an improvement in delivery time.

There would be some routes where overhead clearances would create problems for the additional height of these trailers, but the interstate highway overpasses could accommodate them. If the airfoil provides enough lift to compensate for its drag, and therefore some fuel savings, perhaps newly constructed trailers would be reduced in height to enable them to travel with less restriction. If there is enough volume inside the airfoil to make it worthwhile, it could be filled with helium for a little additional lift. With the prospect of ever-increasing fuel costs, even a slight improvement in mileage might justify exploration of this idea. It might have applications for railroad freight cars as well.

A HEALTHFUL HUNGER FOR A GREAT IDEA IS
THE BEAUTY AND BLESSEDNESS OF LIFE.
—JEAN INGELOW

CHAPTER 51

ENDING THE WARS IN IRAQ, SYRIA, AND AFGHANISTAN WITH THE BIG BOOM

The United States and its allies could end the wars in Iraq, Syria, and Afghanistan with relative ease if they would simply employ a campaign of supersonic warfare. All the supersonic aircraft currently engaged in air operations over the battle areas would be incorporated in an around-the-clock series of sonic booms over selected areas for approximately one week. Soldiers deprived of sleep for this period of time will be ineffective in repulsing an attack by alert, rested forces quickly brought in from areas outside the sonic boom area.

NASA has reported that an aircraft flying supersonic at fifty thousand feet can produce a sonic boom about fifty miles wide. Maximum intensity is directly beneath the aircraft, and it decreases as the lateral distance from the flight path increases. When a supersonic aircraft accelerates to its cruising speed, a focusing effect occurs that makes the sonic boom five to ten times louder than its normal cruising sonic boom over a small region. This effect is similar to how light rays are focused by a lens. Pilots who have assisted NASA in studying sonic booms could instruct the NATO pilots on how to concentrate their sonic booms on specific enemy positions. Sonic booms caused by aircraft flying at very low altitudes will cause glass windows to shatter, with fragments being propelled ten to twelve feet. Flights at these altitudes should be aimed only at clearly identified enemy strongholds.

The best place to test this technique would be a remote mountain valley currently infested with Al Qaeda or Taliban forces. The valley's inhabitants should be informed that anyone who would prefer not to be involved in military action should leave the valley within thirty days of the announcement. The non-Taliban personnel should be offered temporary housing and food outside the valley, perhaps in tents or other easily assembled structures, with the assurance that once the Taliban have been eliminated from the valley they could return to their homes. During the thirty-day period, blocking forces should be established at the valley entrance and other possible exit routes. After the thirty days have elapsed, a campaign would begin during which the valley would be exposed to sonic booms at approximately fifteen-minute intervals around the clock for a period of at least one week. Taliban attempting to escape up the sides of the valley or out through its entrance would be destroyed by a combination of air and ground forces. During this operation the coalition blocking forces would be equipped with earplugs such as those provided to aircraft-carrier flight deck crews and would be relieved on station every eight hours, thus presenting fresh and alert coalition forces to deal with sleep-deprived Taliban.

After about a week of this sonic warfare, coalition forces should be able to flush out and eliminate or capture any Taliban remaining in the valley. Being sleep deprived, they will be incapable of mounting an effective defense. After the valley has been restored to non-Taliban residents, coalition forces would move to another Taliban-infested area and carry out the same sort of campaign. By implementing this concept area by area, always with overwhelming forces both on the ground and in the air, we can eventually clean the Taliban from large areas of the entire country, especially the remote mountain valleys. I've proposed this concept to various commands but to date have received no response from them, although one retired three-star admiral told me "It's a supersonic idea." He said he'd pass it along to some of his friends still on active duty, but I've heard nothing so far.

> I HAVE LEARNED TO USE THE WORD
> "IMPOSSIBLE" WITH THE GREATEST CAUTION.
> —WERNER VON BRAUN

CHAPTER 52

SOLVING THE GREEK FINANCIAL PROBLEM

In order to facilitate its debt bailout, Greece should consider auctioning off or leasing as many of its 169 uninhabited islands as are needed to come up with adequate funds to restore the nation's financial stability. More-solvent nations might be interested in taking over some of these islands as potential tourist destinations for their wealthier citizens. Japan would probably build retirement complexes on some of them for their rapidly increasing number of aging retirees.

Greek investors have lacked the resources to develop these islands, but the new buyers, awash with funds for which they currently find no secure worldwide investment, would quickly develop the infrastructure to turn this relatively isolated real estate into a Mediterranean paradise. Greece would benefit, not only from the cash received but from the expanded economic activity associated with foreign infrastructure development. Even some of the top hedge funds—for example, J. P. Morgan, Bridgewater Associates, Paulson & Co., or even individual billionaires such as Carlos Slim Helu, William Gates III, Warren Buffett, Mark Zuckerberg, and Michael Jordan, to name a few—might participate in the auction action.

> THE PESSIMIST SEES DIFFICULTY IN EVERY OPPORTUNITY. THE OPTIMIST SEES OPPORTUNITY IN EVERY DIFFICULTY.
> —WINSTON CHURCHILL

CHAPTER 53

FLOATING INDUSTRIAL ISLAND

The concept of a floating industrial island is designed to accomplish several objectives:

1. Reduce the amount of floating plastic trash concentrated in the North Pacific Ocean.
2. Recycle this plastic and make it available to industry in the United States, Canada, Japan, and possibly other nations.
3. Provide a floating oil refinery to serve the export of crude oil from North America to Japan and other Asian nations.

    The initial emphasis on this concept should be the benefit to the environment resulting from reducing the vast plastic trash deposit floating in an area of the northern Pacific Ocean reportedly twice the size of Texas. The economic benefits of recycling the plastic into useful products, thus reducing consumption of fossil fuels, are equally important.

The first step in developing this concept should be for the US Environmental Protection Agency to solicit proposals for the design of a large ship capable of harvesting the floating plastic and either compressing it into dense blocks for shipment to shore-based recycling facilities or capable of processing it aboard ship into final recycled products. Once such a ship has been constructed and found capable of harvesting and processing the Pacific plastic trove, similar ships should be built but designed in such a way that they could be attached to each other at sea as modules, forming the base for a large-area platform capable of supporting additional industry such as an oil refinery.

Since each of these ships would probably be diesel powered, the whole platform could be moved around the ocean at a low speed, facilitating storm avoidance.

The participation of other nations or even the United Nations might be advisable. Since the United States and other nations are reluctant to allow construction of new oil refineries, the floating Pacific industrial island could play an important role in this part of the world economy as well.

THERE IS NOTHING IN THE WORLD REALLY BENEFICIAL THAT DOES NOT LIE WITHIN THE REACH OF AN INFORMED UNDERSTANDING AND A WELL-PROTECTED PURSUIT.
—EDMUND BURKE

CHAPTER 54

ELECTRICITY FROM HIGH-RISE WASTEWATER

Electricity could be produced from the fall of wastewater in high-rise buildings. By channeling the wastewater into one or more pipes that would pass it through a turbine near the ground floor, a considerable amount of electric power could be generated. This power could supplement the normal power supply for the building and would also provide short-term emergency electricity during power outages.

The hydroelectric turbine would have to be designed with more space between blades than regular water turbines, in order to accommodate the solid waste that would make up part of the descending force. Bypass pipes would be available to come online, should the turbine need maintenance. In that many high-rise buildings have very significant electric power costs, this supplementary source should contribute appreciably to reducing the overall cost of operating the building. As a concomitant feature, the solid waste could be allowed to slide into a tank, where it would produce methane that could be used in heating and cooling the building, with the residue converted into fertilizer for the city's parks.

THE MOST EXCITING PHRASE TO HEAR IN SCIENCE, THE ONE THAT HERALDS NEW DISCOVERIES, IS NOT "EUREKA!," BUT "THAT'S FUNNY."

—ISAAC ASIMOV

CHAPTER 55

EXPEDITING OFF-LOADING OF CONTAINER SHIPS

Many container ships are kept at anchor for days, awaiting space alongside a pier equipped for off-loading. This results in considerable expense for all involved in the process and in lost sales for products that could have been sold profitably had on-time delivery been possible. This problem could be partially alleviated by off-loading the top layer or two of containers by heavy-lift helicopters or lighter-than-air vehicles. Terminals equipped for air delivery could be developed with good rail and highway access, thus avoiding the congestion near seaports.

> THERE ARE BASICALLY TWO TYPES OF PEOPLE. PEOPLE WHO ACCOMPLISH THINGS, AND PEOPLE WHO CLAIM TO HAVE ACCOMPLISHED THINGS. THE FIRST GROUP IS LESS CROWDED.
> —MARK TWAIN

CHAPTER 56

COUNTERING ILLEGAL IMMIGRATION

The United States should enact a law making illegal immigrants subject to a fine of $250,000. Apprehended illegal immigrants unable to pay this fine would be moved to comfortable barracks in a well-guarded industrial zone where they would work producing items currently being imported from China but not manufactured in the United States, Canada, or Mexico. They would be paid at the same rate the Chinese pay for this type of work, and after deducting the amount required to house and feed them, their earnings would be applied to the $250,000 fine they have incurred.

In certain parts of the country where forest fires and brush fires are frequent, teams of these immigrants would be used to clear swaths of endangered areas, converting this vegetation into charcoal for export to countries where charcoal is a popular product or shipping it to coal-burning power plants. There it would be combined with coal, thus reducing the emissions of acid rain–producing sulfur dioxide, smog-forming nitrous oxide, fly ash, uranium, and thorium. Once they have paid off their fine, they would be eligible for nonresident-alien status. Illegal immigrants trying to escape from the industrial zone would be imprisoned and later delivered to the country from which they had left prior to arriving in the United States. These deliveries could be made at remote locations on the coastline of this nation. Workers in the industrial zone who learn English and exhibit good work performance would be given better-paying jobs, allowing them to pay off their fines earlier than would be the case with less-productive workers. For example, if some of the illegal immigrants have skills that can be employed effectively within the industrial zone, such as doctors, dentists, computer programmers, engineers, teachers, electricians, plumbers, carpenters, masons, mechanics, or other technicians, they would be given appropriate salaries and pay off their fines expeditiously. Families would be provided adequate housing, minors would be provided schooling, and all immigrants would be provided medical care. Some of the immigrants would be given jobs producing food, clothing, and other necessities; however, their production would be consumed only within the industrial zone, so as not to compete with producers outside the zone.

The immigrants would not be allowed to send any of their earnings out of the country. All of their earnings would be used only to pay the $250,000 fine. Illegal immigrants capable of paying the $250,000 fine when apprehended would be obligated to work for two years in the industrial zones. A comprehensive campaign should be conducted in the nations from which the majority of illegal immigrants come, explaining this new law and its consequences for illegal immigrants. Once the word gets out that illegal immigration to the United States would result in this form of law enforcement, the number of illegal immigrants is very likely to drop substantially.

In conjunction with the implementation of this plan, a much more comprehensive campaign imposing large fines on employers of illegal immigrants should be enforced, and an additional plan for allowing legal but temporary employment for agricultural harvesters should be put in place. The products being produced in these industrial zones will replace significant numbers of these same products now being imported, thus improving the balance of trade. The anti–forest fire and brushfire efforts carried out by these teams will reduce annual losses from and costs of fighting these fires; the cost of patrolling borders and apprehending and imprisoning illegal immigrants will be reduced; and crime associated with the coyote system of illegal immigration will decline. Illegal immigration will always be a problem, but with the implementation of the above-listed actions, it will become far more manageable.

A NATION THAT CANNOT CONTROL ITS BORDERS IS NOT A NATION.
—RONALD REAGAN

CHAPTER 57

A SERVICE THAT COULD BE PROVIDED BY STREET BEGGARS

Beggars on the city streets could perform a useful service and at the same time be reimbursed for their efforts by presenting a sign similar to this one and following through on the offer when paid.

"Your breath can lead to a new job,
a pleasing conversation, a kiss,
and even more;
or it can destroy such possibilities.
I'll evaluate yours for $1."

Many beggars are delivered to their begging sites by a syndicate. It won't take long for the syndicates to implement this service, once they learn about it from this book.

NEVER STAND BEGGING FOR THAT WHICH YOU HAVE THE POWER TO EARN.
—MIGUEL DE CERVANTES

CHAPTER 58

FILLING EMPTY COAL CARS WITH GARBAGE TO BE DUMPED IN ABANDONED MINES

Empty coal cars could be filled with garbage from the cities through which they pass on their return to mines in the West. The garbage could then be dumped into abandoned mines, where the rock structure would be adequate for safely containing the landfill. The money received from the cities for the disposal of their garbage could be used to develop landfills in appropriate mine areas. The new landfills in these areas could also provide methane gas for nearby communities.

> PEOPLE'S MINDS ARE CHANGED THROUGH OBSERVATION AND NOT THROUGH ARGUMENT.
>
> —WILL ROGERS

EPILOGUE

Chapter 1, in one form or another, has been submitted to both executive and legislative branches of the US government, to appropriate departments at the United Nations, and to a variety of world leaders. To date, there have been no responses, so I am considering developing an organization to get the concept implemented. Readers who would be interested in participating in such an organization should contact me at cconger6@gmail.com. Here is a typical letter I've submitted to officials I thought might be willing to support and explore the idea.

June 23, 2015
His Holiness, Pope Francis
Apostolic Palace
00120 Vatican City
Your Holiness:

I have a concept that you could assist in implementing worldwide that would stand as a positive contribution to the improvement of humanity and the world environment, unequaled by any individual in recent history. It fits well with your recent efforts to combat global warming and at the same time will disarm your critics who fear that your interest in defeating global warming will have a serious impact on the near-term world economy, so dependent on the consumption of fossil fuels.

Millions of workers, managers, and owners of businesses dependent to a substantial degree on the combustion of fossil fuels are terrified at the prospect that their livelihood is about to be destroyed by environmentalists. These businesses have spent billions of dollars and are planning on spending hundreds of billions more in efforts to reduce the production of carbon dioxide and other greenhouse gases that are blamed by many authorities for the earth's current warming cycle that began in 1850. But you can promote a solution to the problem of global warming that will be far less expensive and far more effective than any plan currently in effect or on the drawing boards.

Beginning in the 1940s, there had been a slight interruption in the general warming cycle. A few meteorologists and climatologists and many alarmists eager to attach themselves to the latest looming disaster feared the return of the Little Ice Age, a global cooling cycle that occurred between 1580 and 1850.

Many climatologists believe the warming and cooling of the earth is affected by changes in the sun's output, with periods of high solar flare or sunspot activity. These could be followed by warm periods on the earth and periods of low sunspot activity followed by cool periods. Other scientists believe that since these changes occur more frequently than changes in relatively long warming or cooling cycles, they are less likely to cause long-term change than other phenomena such as changes in the earth's orbit around the sun, changes in the inclination of the earth toward the sun, and changes in the earth's magnetic poles. A few authorities think tectonic plate activity, particularly on the floor of the Pacific Ocean, resulting in extrusions of quantities of molten lava has some effect, possibly causing the warm periods called El Niño and the cool periods, La Niña. Still others believe that greenhouse effects caused by stratospheric concentrations of carbon dioxide and other gases are to blame. There is less agreement on whether human activity causes these cycles, but an increasing number of scientists and other students of weather trends believe that the warming trend evident since 1850 has been influenced by a greenhouse effect intensified by the burning of fossil fuels.

Regardless of the basic cause of global cooling, it appears that a cooling trend begins with a series of winters in which there is an early and extensive snowfall in the Northern Hemisphere. With a greater-than-usual area of the land covered by snow, more of the sun's rays are reflected back into space rather than absorbed by the bare ground. This process, referred to in scientific circles as albedo, results in approximately 90 percent of the sun's rays being reflected from the snow back into space. After several winters of increasingly cold temperatures over increasingly longer periods of time, each long winter seems to replicate itself in a sort of snowball effect. Then the snowfields and glaciers expand and a cooling cycle begins.

Now, with the threat of global warming replacing the potential calamity of global cooling, I began to think that by sending more of the sun's rays back into space, we could slow or even stop global warming.

My current idea is to cover a substantial area of undeveloped land as well as agricultural fields around the world with a thin coat of lime, white sand, kaolin, a reflective polyethylene mulch, or other white nontoxic substance, thus replicating the effect of an early snowfall. The white substances would have definite advantages over an early snowfall in their ability to reflect sunlight. Unlike snow, these substances would not disappear in the spring. If lime were used for this purpose, it would eventually be absorbed into the soil or washed into waterways, then replaced as necessary.

Since thousands of acres of farmland and forests are currently degraded from the effects of acid rain, absorption of lime would be beneficial, not only to the fields being treated but to streams, ponds, and lakes receiving the resultant alkaline runoff. Many of these waterways are so acidic today that they are no longer inhabited by fish and other wildlife dependent on them. The states of New York and West Virginia and sportsmen's clubs and other organizations interested in reclaiming streams and ponds in the United States Northeast, have already been adding lime directly to streams and ponds to counter the ill effects of acid rain.

Spreading lime or other white substances over agricultural land after it has been seeded, but just before the plants have sprouted, thus not interfering with germination, may have other beneficial effects. Because the sun's rays striking the white surface would be reflected outward at various angles, rather than being absorbed in the untreated earth, the emerging plants would receive a double dose of sunlight. Experiments have shown that plants that have received greater-than-normal exposure to ultraviolet rays are less susceptible to attack by insects. A reflective polyethylene mulch is already being applied to the soil in a few fruit orchards in the United States in order to achieve a more uniform ripe coloring of the fruit through the reflected sun rays.

Additional reflected sunlight could not only help plants resist insects but accelerate the process of photosynthesis, causing them to mature more quickly, lessening the time of exposure to hungry herbivores and omnivores, drought, hailstorms, and early fall freezes, and possibly have favorable impacts on crop yields. In areas where lime is determined to be an undesirable component to the soil, another white, insoluble and nontoxic substance could be applied. A similar nontoxic substance able to float on water in powder, granular, or liquid form could be spread over large deep-water ocean areas with little effect on submerged vegetation but would reflect the sun's rays back into space. This would allow these ocean areas to remain cooler than would otherwise be the case. This same substance applied to rice paddies at an appropriate time might give rice plants enough extra photosynthesis to mature more quickly with the same benefits outlined above for grains grown on dry land.

Concomitant benefits from spreading a white film over ocean areas might result in fewer and weaker hurricanes and typhoons. Some scientists have speculated that the intensity of recent hurricanes may have been increased by higher-than-usual temperatures in the Gulf of Mexico. Some of the cooling efforts I have in mind might even reduce the threat of tornadoes (more on this later).

It might take several years to determine the effect these techniques have on global warming, but effects of the acid-reducing lime applications would provide near-term benefits. International participation in this program would provide earlier evidence of its efficacy. Since acid rain is a problem in both Europe and Asia, the lime application would begin immediately to alleviate damage to the environment caused by acid rain.

Other techniques for reflecting sunlight could be applied in conjunction with the ground-whitening process. Roofs of both residential and commercial buildings could be painted white, adding to the reduction in heat-absorbing surfaces. Incentives such as income tax deductibility or tax credits could be initiated to encourage whitening of both ground and rooftop surfaces. The state of California in the United States has already made some progress in this area.

I have nothing against the various schemes designed to reduce the emissions of carbon dioxide and to improve air quality, but I think the scientists and their followers who propose them are attacking the symptoms of the problem rather than the problem itself.

Symptoms of the problem are warm gaseous particles in the atmosphere that have been transformed into their current heated state from a cooler existence on the earth's surface through collisions with particles speeding from the sun's core at the speed of light. If all combustion of fossil fuels suddenly came to a halt, global warming would still continue, unless something is done to prevent so many of the sun's high-speed particles from transforming less-aggressive earth particles into hot little components of the atmosphere. This can be done easily by whitening significant areas of the earth so that like the snow cover in winter, they can reflect these high-speed, global warming particles back into space before inflicting their damage on the earth.

I have been trying for several years to interest the US federal government, the United Nations, and other entities capable of implementing this plan for countering global warming, with no response. So without governmental assistance in whitening the earth, I've tried to develop incentives for independent participation by owners of land areas and other surfaces that could be whitened. If farmers and others engaged in agriculture can be convinced that whitening their fields will be cost effective, they might be willing to adopt this practice. A concomitant benefit could accompany any significant application of whitening to agricultural fields. Since whitened ground would be cooler than the presumably larger areas of adjacent untreated ground, a weather condition similar to the coastal sea breeze effect should develop. With the cooler air above the whitened fields moving outward toward the untreated fields, warmer air above these fields would rise. Depending on the extent of the whitened fields, the cool breezes thus produced might inhibit the forming of tornadoes. A small town, with all its roofs painted white, surrounded by acres of whitened fields, might be less vulnerable to tornadoes.

The American president Theodore Roosevelt frequently noted the importance of "the Bully Pulpit," a sufficiently conspicuous position that provides an opportunity to speak out and be listened to. He referred to the White House as a "bully pulpit," by which he meant a terrific platform from which to advocate an agenda. Roosevelt used the word *bully* as an adjective meaning "superb" or "wonderful," a more common usage in his time than it is today.

You have a far more wonderful pulpit than he did, and if you used it to implement this plan for fighting global warming, the world would benefit enormously.

I realize that this idea will encounter considerable skepticism. John Locke predicted quite eloquently, "New opinions are always suspected and usually opposed, without any other reason but because they are not already common."

But if the concept turns out to have potential for reducing global warming, hurricanes, and tornadoes, and the effects of acid rain as well, it would eventually find support from those currently impacted by these effects, especially those living in areas where a future rising sea level can expect to have disastrous economic and social effects. Every industrial and individual consumer of fossil fuel stands to benefit from this concept through the relaxation of costly efforts to slow the greenhouse effect. Concomitant improvements in agricultural productivity and wildlife habitat constitute an additional bonus.

THE TIME HAS COME TO WHITEN THE EARTH.
I AM, YOUR HOLINESS, MOST RESPECTFULLY
YOURS IN CHRIST,

CLAYTON NED CONGER

C.N. Conger
Ruiz de Alarcón 7
Madrid, 28014 Spain
cconger6@gmail.com
Telephone 001 703 507 6246
June 23, 2015

Msgr. Fabián Pedacchio Leániz
Apostolic Palace
00120 Vatican City
Dear Msgr. Pedacchio:

For many years I have been studying the problem of global warming and have tried to interest government authorities in a concept I've developed to counter this phenomenon. These efforts have generally been unsuccessful, but now with the interest expressed in the subject by Pope Francis, I'm hoping to inspire him to put his global influence behind a campaign that I'm quite sure will be successful. I'm enclosing a letter to Pope Francis that you might provide to him if appropriate. I think he will like it and implement it.

With his encouragement, millions of parishioners will begin to whiten the earth, some of them on an individual basis and others through governmental and commercial organizations. Jobs capable of being filled by the millions of unemployed men and women will be created throughout the world.

Since this program will begin to slow global warming, other far more expensive measures can be implemented more slowly with less impact on the users of fossil fuels.

I'm sure that you know experts that can evaluate this concept. Unfortunately many of them are so dedicated to the fight against the use of fossil fuels that they have no interest in any other effort to combat global warming. But by implementing the earth-whitening concept and making progress in cooling the earth, the transition to alternative energy sources can be accomplished with less economic disruption and without undue confrontation between environmentalists and fossil fuel users.

Very respectfully,
Ned Conger

Clayton Ned Conger
Ruiz de Alarcón 7
Madrid, 28014
Spain
cconger6@gmail.com
001 703 507 6246

www.ingramcontent.com/pod-product-compliance
Lightning Source LLC
Chambersburg PA
CBHW020521290526
45786CB00002B/702